The Shell Book of Beachcombing

The Shell Book of
Beachcombing

Tony Soper

With illustrations by
Robert Gillmor

DAVID & CHARLES
NEWTON ABBOT

BY THE SAME AUTHOR

The Bird Table Book

with John Sparks
Penguins
Owls

with Frank Booker and Crispin Gill
The Wreck of the *Torrey Canyon*

For my fellow beachcombers
bug, beast and man alike
but most of all for Hilary

ISBN 0 7153 5799 9

© *TONY SOPER 1972*

First edition 1972
Reprinted 1973

Set in 12/13 Centaur
and printed in Great Britain
by Fletcher & Son Ltd Norwich
for David & Charles (Holdings) Limited
South Devon House Newton Abbot Devon

Contents

Illustrations

Chapter headings also by Robert Gillmor
Tail pieces by Thomas Bewick

Introduction

If you are good at it, you can make a living from the seashore. Eating fish soup, sea beet and cockles, and picking up lost coinage and diamond rings, not to mention pieces-of-eight, to pay for your visits to civilisation. But most of us go wrecking for fun, and because we never know what might be round the next corner. In some parts of the country it is in the blood, and men have actually come to blows in the struggle to be first into a promising cave as the tide falls back. Some get up before dawn to be first on the tideline. Some do it the lazy way and drive a Landrover from end to end of the beach in a few minutes, making a lot of noise in the process.

Jellyfish, pit props, fish-boxes and far flung timber riddled with ship worm and covered with goose barnacles; the list of possibilities is endless, including everything from a tropical bean to a grand piano. The seashore is the most rewarding of all habitats.

1 Coastal forces

This book is about a battleground. The coastline is a theatre of war between two great opposing forces—land and sea. Here the sea gains ground, reducing cliffs to rubble and sweeping away the debris; there the land wins, as silt and sand slowly build up on tidal mud-flats and sand dunes. It is a never-ending conflict, and as the fortunes of war favour one side or the other, the front-line beach changes in turn. It is a violent sort of place, never at rest, never the same two days running. Yet there is a wonderful exhilaration in patrolling it, and on calm quiet days a rare peace.

Nowadays the coast is subject to increasing pressure from a third force, man himself. If all of us in England and Wales went to the coast there would not be enough room to stand there, with only four inches of shoulder room for each. And if we took our cars with us they would be five-deep. More than a quarter of our entire coast is developed or about to be developed; but the National Trust and con-servation bodies hold some 15 per cent of the coastal frontage in protective ownership, and we still have access to the half-million acres of British seashore.

To enjoy it to the full, it is good to have some idea of the nature of the sea forces which play so large a part in shaping the shore. A beachcomber needs to know about the weather, and he needs to know about tidal times and rhythms to make effective use of his time. A good onshore wind may throw any quantity of wreck onto a beach, and maybe it is only at low water that the best parts of your foreshore can be reached.

Tides with the greatest range, covering most and revealing most in turn, are spring tides, reaching their peak at the time of new and full moons. Tides with the least range, and the least covering and revealing movement, are neaps, occurring at the moon's quarters. An easy and useful rule of thumb for calculating sea-level at any moment is to remember that the rate of change is one-twelfth of the range in the first and sixth hours, two-twelfths in the second and fifth hours and three-twelfths in the third and fourth hours. That is to say the water rises (or falls) fastest at half-tide. But this rough rule has to be greatly modified in places like the Solent, where the double tides well and truly confuse the issue. Times of high and low water are best discovered from the cheap pocket tide-tables which you will get from your nearest chandler or fishing-tackle shop. The range is the difference between high and low water on any given day, and we must soon learn to think of it in metres.

Weather conditions have quite significant effects on the height of tide. Extremes of atmospheric pressure or strong steady winds may lower or raise the predicted height by as much as a foot (or a third of a metre if you prefer it!); winds may advance or delay the actual time of high water as compared with predicted time. This effect is most noticeable in any kind of bottleneck situation, for example an estuary, where high water may be sustained by as much as an hour when an onshore wind holds the sea high up. Wind raises sea-level in the direction it is blowing, so a strong wind blowing directly on-shore will pile up the water and cause sea-levels higher than pre-dicted.

A low atmospheric pressure will tend to raise sea-level and a high pressure will depress it. A change of 1in in the barometer reading indicates a variation of about 1ft in the height of sea-level, and that is about as great a change as is ever likely.

12

In the southern part of the North Sea, storm surges may cause tides to vary as much as 3ft from predicted heights, and even greater variations may occur in the Thames estuary. These surges are usually caused by deep depressions moving east across the northern part of the North Sea; they are the result of an oscillating effect caused by rapid changes of weather. In other parts of Great Britain this oscillating effect on sea-level produces a wave effect known as a Seiche. They may have a height of anything from an inch or so up to several feet, and the period between waves may be anything between a few minutes and a couple of hours. Small Seiches are not uncommon, especially in certain harbours, for instance Fishguard and Wick. They can cause a great deal of damage when they are unexpected.

Weather information is really very important to the intending beachcomber, and it is as well to know your local sources. Meteorological offices give excellent short-term forecasts by telephone; you can find the number in the opening pages of the telephone directory. The BBC coastal waters forecast is useful, and you get a glimpse of a pressure and wind chart on television in the evening. Then on BBC Radio 2 on 1500m (200 kHz), there is a general synopsis and 24-hour forecast at 0202, 0640, 1355 (1155 on Sundays) and 1757.

If you want to try your hand at your own weather forecasting you will need a barometer. But remember that single readings are not of much value. It is no good giving it a knowing tap as you walk out of the door, because unless you have been giving it a whole series of knowing taps you will not know what the trend is. Weather forecasting with a barometer is nothing if it's not trendy.

The arrival of a gale is often forecast by a fall of pressure and by the wind backing (i.e. changing direction anti-clockwise). The actual change of pressure may be a fairly rapid process, but the gale itself may be delayed a considerable time after the barometer indication. Steady or rising pressure when the pressure is already high is a likely indicator of quiet weather. Even if there are high winds at this time, they are unlikely to arrive suddenly; they will gradually increase in strength. After unsettled weather, a rising barometer probably forecasts better conditions.

It is very easy to make a crude 'beach barometer', but while it is an amusing thing to have, one has to admit its forecasting value is not great. First, as Mrs Beeton would say, catch yourself a chianti bottle. Naturally, it's best to find one on the shoreline, but a bottle bought from the wine merchant has a built-in advantage. After you've drunk the advantage, tear off the straw basket so that you're left with the naked bottle (and, incidentally, a red chianti bottle is more suitable than a white wine one). Now you need a Kilner jar. Fill the jar with water. Invert the empty (and clean and dry) chianti bottle and fit it into the Kilner jar. Take out water from the Kilner jar until the water comes up to cover the thick part (where the cork used to be) of the chianti bottle. The device, which is pressure controlled and depends on the locked air contained in the upturned bottle, may take several days to settle down. But, in due course, you will be able to observe atmospheric pressure changes indicated by the rising and falling of the water-level inside the neck of the wine bottle. Keep it away from direct sunlight and in ordinary room temperature. Last of all, to get full value from the gadget, and further confuse your visitors, you must explain what it means. My friend Joanna Pickett who runs an office for the BBC's Natural History Unit, has a typed notice on her bottle-forecaster. It says 'This is a weather forecaster! The higher the water rises in the neck of the bottle, the better the weather will be. When the top of the bottle gets steamy, mist or light rain is due; and when the top gets full of heavy condensation, it foretells heavy rain. Sometimes the water in the neck of the bottle is "blown" out, and a heavy storm is imminent.'

To go with your home-made barometer, you might like to remember the old seamen's rhymes, which are good advice, nine times out of ten:

> Long foretold, long last,
> Short notice, soon past,
> Quick rise after low,
> Sure sign of stronger blow.

When the glass falls low
Prepare for a blow;
When it slowly rises high,
Lofty canvas you may fly.

At sea with low and falling glass,
Soundly sleeps a careless ass,
Only when it's high and rising,
Truly rests a careful wise one.

The evening red and morning grey
Are sure signs of a fine day,
But the evening grey and the morning red,
Makes the sailor shake his head.

Mackerel sky and mares' tails,
Make lofty ships carry low sails.

The traditional piece of weather-forecasting seaweed offers a crude measure of humidity. When the seaweed becomes damp, rain is imminent. But, sadly, it is not a very reliable forecaster. If you want to try it, then the right species of kelp to use is *Laminaria saccharina*, the one with a long (anything up to 8 ft) undivided wavy frond, yellowy olive with a smooth cylindrical stalk and attached to stones and rocks by the root-like structures of a hold-fast.

BEAUFORT WIND SCALE

Beaufort wind force	Mean wind speed in knots	Descriptive terms	Sea criterion	Probable height of waves in feet
0	less than 1	calm	Sea like a mirror	—
1	1–3	light air	ripples with the appearance of scales are formed but without foam crests.	$\frac{1}{4}$
2	4–6	light breeze	Small wavelets, still short but more pronounced. Crests have a glassy appearance and do not break.	$\frac{1}{2}$
3	7–10	gentle breeze	Large wavelets. Crests begin to break. Foam of glassy appearance. Perhaps scattered white horses.	2
4	11–16	moderate breeze	Small waves, becoming longer. Fairly frequent white horses.	$3\frac{1}{2}$
5	17–21	fresh breeze	Moderate waves, taking a more pronounced long form. Many white horses formed. (Chance of some spray.)	6
6	22–27	strong breeze	Large waves begin to form. White foam crests more extensive everywhere. (Probably some spray.)	$9\frac{1}{2}$
7	28–33	near gale	Sea heaps up and white foam from breaking waves begins to be blown in streaks along the direction of the wind.	$13\frac{1}{2}$
8	34–40	gale	Moderately high waves of greater length. Edges of	18

			crests begin to break into spindrift. The foam is blown in well-marked streaks along the direction of the wind.	
9	41–47	strong gale	High waves. Dense streaks of foam along the direction of the wind. Crests of waves begin to topple, tumble and roll over. Spray may affect visibility.	23
10	48–55	storm	Very high waves with long overhanging crests. The resulting foam in great patches is blown in dense white streaks along the direction of the wind. On the whole the surface of the sea takes a white appearance. The tumbling of the sea becomes heavy and shocklike. Visibility affected.	29
11	56–63	violent storm	Exceptionally high waves. (Small and medium-sized ships might be for a time lost to view behind the waves.) The sea is completely covered with long white patches of foam lying along the direction of the wind. Everywhere the edges of the wave crests are blown into froth. Visibility affected.	37
12	64+	hurricane	The air is filled with foam and spray. Sea completely white with driving spray. Visibility very seriously affected.	45

Currents and tidal streams are phenomena of enormous interest to the beachcomber. A knowledge of the local surface movements of sea water and the way in which they relate to ocean currents is vital if we are to say with any certainty where 'wreck' has come from, and even more importantly, when it is likely to be cast ashore, in prevailing weather conditions.

Sea water expands and contracts in seasonal cycles. Along with the effect of constant winds, this results in ocean movements. Their direction is influenced by the earth's rotation; and in the northern hemisphere the general circulation is in a clockwise direction (like the whirlpool in your bath). In the North Atlantic this sea-current revolves round the Azores' 'High', the more or less permanent anti-cyclone system. And the result, which is of immense importance to

Various 'drifters'. The right-hand bottle is a surface-current floater, ballasted so that the top is just awash, minimising direct wind influence. The coconut and the left-hand bottle are bottom drifters. The coconut is holed and sinks to the bottom; the bottle is carefully ballasted in the neck and the copper wire straightened out before release so that on reaching the bottom the bottle rests lightly poised on the tip of the wire and dances along under the influence of sea-bed currents.

OIL POLLUTION INVESTIGATION
National Institute of Oceanography CARD № .

Name and address of finder
Nome e endereço do achador
Nombre y dirección de la persona que lo
Votre nom et votre adresse   [encontró
Naam en adres van de vinder
Name und Anschrift des Finders
Finderens navn og adresse

Place at which envelope was found
Local em que foi achado o sobrescrito
Lugar en que fué hallado
Lieu où l'enveloppe a été trouvée
Plaats waar de enveloppe gevonden werd
Wo wurde der Umschlag gefunden?
Stedet, hvor konvolutten blev fundet
Stedet hvor konvolutten blev funnet

Date when envelope was found
Data em que foi achado o sobrescrito
Fecha del hallazgo
Date de la trouvaille
Datum waarop de envelop gevonden werd
Wann wurde der Umschlag gefunden?
Dato, da konvolutten blev fundet
Dato da konvolutten blev funnet

Drift postcard in plastic envelope

all beachcombers, is that the Gulf Stream, of tropical origin, works its way up the eastern seaboard of North America, then travels east across the Atlantic to become the North Atlantic Current, losing strength and splitting into two parts, one of which flows northwards past Scotland and one of which flows east to the English Channel and the Bay of Biscay. Now we know why it is that Caribbean plant seeds sometimes end up on west-coast beaches—and sometimes great quantities of exotic jellyfish.

Changes in wind speed and direction alter the nature of this great current, and the resulting maverick movements are known as the North Atlantic Drift. In coastal waters local currents are influenced by the effects of rain, tidal streams and the local geography.

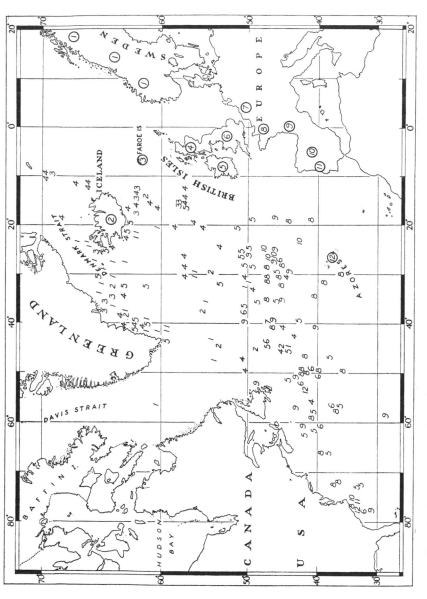

Some drift-bottle journeys made good in the North Atlantic. From the positions marked by numerals, bottles have beached on the coasts of countries marked with matching circled numerals.

Charting the course of these currents has involved the release of many thousands of drift bottles and, more recently, plastic drift envelopes. They are used by organisations interested in currents and tides. For instance, the Ministry of Agriculture Fisheries and Food, and the Marine Biological Association want to know about plankton and fish movements in relation to sea movements; industrialists wish to trace the likely course of effluent and chemical waste when it is dumped at sea.

In 1954 the National Institute of Oceanography organised a massive drop of plastic drift envelopes. Sunderlands of Royal Air Force Coastal Command flew from Pembroke Dock and released some 9,000 envelopes between the Bay of Biscay and the Faeroes. The heavy plastic envelopes contained postcards requesting information about date and recovery position. Previous experience in Australian and South African waters had shown that these surface-drifters were susceptible to attack by albatross and other seabirds. So in this experiment a thin sheet of cork was enclosed with the postcard, to give added buoyancy. The cards were dropped in bundles of ten, loosely bound with a disintegrating tape, at four and a half minute intervals, that is, every 10 miles along the track. A reward of half-a-crown ($12\frac{1}{2}$p) was offered to the finder.

The results were highly successful. Eighteen months after the drop over 2,500 cards had been returned to the Institute, representing a 40 per cent recovery rate. (This figure excludes one drop, which was a total failure for technical reasons.) The envelopes were returned by beachcombers working the coasts between southern Portugal and northern Scandinavia. Some of the cards were fresh and clean, some were dog-eared and faded, some pulped and almost unreadable. Yet of all the cards returned, only one was so disintegrated that the vital serial number was unreadable.

One thousand three hundred and twenty-seven of the cards beached on the shores of the British Isles, twice as many as on other coasts (see page 19). The result was not surprising, but it confirmed the expected flow of the North Atlantic Drift. More than half of the British cards were returned from the remoter parts of the Scottish Islands, over 200 of them coming from Shetland. None at all were found between the Firth of Forth and the Thames estuary, and only a few from the north west, a result which showed, not surprisingly, that those stretches of coastline are relatively unaffected by ocean currents. Three of the cards were retrieved from Portugal, but the most exciting recovery was of a card which had travelled all the way to the Rybachi Peninsula in the Barents Sea, just inside the Russian border.

The experiment showed that floating objects in the sea area off the British Isles between Biscay and the Faeroes tend to strand somewhere on the shores of north-west Europe influenced by prevailing wind conditions, and that the odds are very much in favour of such objects landing on British or Irish beaches. It is clear that wind conditions are very important in predicting the course made good by floating 'wreck'.

Surface ocean currents are mirrored by underwater currents which are normally on a reciprocal course, and there are drift devices which are designed to plot underwater currents in much the same way that surface currents are traced. But the device, since it must first sink and then jog along the sea bed, looks rather different from the simple postcard in a plastic envelope. Much of the sea-bed current research has taken place in the southern North Sea, using specially weighted glass bottles. But nowadays the favoured transport is the 'Woodhead sea-bed drifter', a gaily-coloured plastic mushroom, with a 7 gram copper weight crimped to the bottom of its 'stalk' (see page 24).

Since 1960 over 15,000 have been released. In much the same way as the plastic surface-drift envelopes, the sea-bed drifters are released in bundles, tied with a soluble film attached to a bag of gravel. When the film dissolves after about 20 minutes, the saucer mushrooms stand up and drift off wherever the current takes them. A numbered polythene tag is attached to the saucer, with the legend '5/- reward for drifter, tag and full details'. On the saucer itself is an embossed message in several languages, asking the finder to inform his Fishery Officer, or the Fisheries Laboratory at Lowestoft. Many of the drifters are caught in trawl nets, but many of them escape capture this way and end up on beaches. The recovery rate is very satisfactory. Of 2,000 drifters released in spring 1960 south of the Dogger Bank, 48

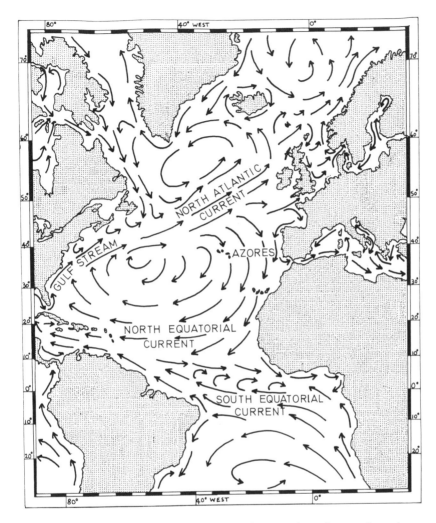

General surface-current circulation of the North Atlantic (based on Admiralty Chart 5310 with the sanction of the Controller, HMSO and of the Hydrographer of the Navy).

Woodhead drifters on the seabed

per cent had been returned within one year; 11 per cent of these came from beaches. Subsequent experiments have confirmed the same pattern.

On 1 May 1972 the Mental Health Research Fund launched 'Operation Mayday', a sponsored sea-current experiment in which a number of drifters was released in the North Sea. Each drifter was sponsored at a cost of £25, and carried a label identifying the name of the sponsor and the London address to which it should be returned. Although there is no reward, the beachcomber will be helping a worthy cause by returning the label. Success with these investigations obviously depends a great deal on the co-operation of both fishermen and beachcombers, but it is not surprising that people are willing to go to the small trouble of returning a drifter; there is a sense of romance and mystery about these frail objects, carrying their tell-tale number tag—the key to information about their wanderings. And, of course, there is often a reward!

The practice of sealing messages into a bottle and casting it to the sea in the hope that someone somewhere will recover it is very long-established. Not only serious oceanographers use the sea-post. It is not easy to be sure when the practice began. Certainly the British ship *Rainbow* put out floating bottles in 1802 to test currents, but continental researchers put the date as early as 1763; these dates relate to the scientific use of bottle-post. Bernardin de Saint-Pierre, writing in 1784, claims that Christopher Columbus, when in danger of perishing in a mid-Atlantic tempest, consigned an account of his discoveries to a barrel which he committed to the waves in the hope that it would arrive sooner or later on a beach.

Following a boatman's discovery of a vital political secret (that Novya Zemlya had been seized from Russia by the Dutch) contained in a bottle message picked up on the beach at Dover, Queen Elizabeth in 1560 appointed an official Uncorker of Bottles. Any unauthorised person who let his curiosity get the better of him in the matter of opening stranded messenger bottles was liable to hang. The Crown appointment lapsed in the reign of George III: just as well perhaps.

In the mid-nineteenth century it was a common thing for floating bottles with papers inside to be flung overboard from outward bound emigrant ships. Very often, after a seagoing party, a motley collection of bottles (empty) would dance along the wake carrying jovial messages, usually with spurious news of shipwreck and disaster.

The practice of using drift bottles and other buoyant message containers for serious oceanographical research is long-established and still going strong today. An empty bottle will drift largely under the influence of wind and to determine surface sea currents the bottle is ballasted with a carefully calculated amount of sand. Usually there is also a questionnaire postcard printed in several languages, an information slip and an easily-seen label asking the finder to break the bottle and take the first step towards his reward. One side of the card is printed with a return address. If all the questions are answered, then the researcher will know where and when a bottle began and ended its journey. Time actually spent afloat is not so easily determined, because of course a bottle may have lain on the beach undiscovered for some time. But, over a period of time, it is possible to make a fairly accurate assessment. Finders of British bottles usually get a reward of 15 pence or so, and the satisfaction of having done their bit towards ocean research. Over the years, drift experiments have done a great deal towards establishing the pattern of sea surface and bottom movements. For instance, Dr Fulton's research in the years 1894–7 for the Fishery Board of Scotland established the existence of a great cyclonic surface-current system in the North Sea. This work has been continued and, based on Aberdeen, some 3,000 bottles a year are sown in North Sea waters. Some of the recovery percentages are remarkable; of 4,825 bottles liberated between 1910–14, 22·8 per cent were recovered; better still, from a long series of weekly releases in the southern North Sea, Dr J. N. Carruthers recovered no less than 6,435 cards, representing a recovery rate of 67·4 per cent. Researchers in the Bay of Biscay commonly achieve a return of 30 per cent, although on occasion it has been as high as 66 per cent.

Over the years a surprising variety of message-carrying floaters has been used—barrels, cylinders, spheres, buoys, tubes, etc., and even coconut shells! Very often bottles and envelopes have been retrieved by fishermen, while they were still at sea. Records like this are very useful in filling the gaps and giving more information about the path the bottles are following on their way to shore.

Sometimes the bottles travel great distances and wait long periods for discovery. One was released by Dr W. S. Bruce of the Scottish Antarctic Expedition of 1902–4, in the Southern Ocean, east of Cape Horn, and discovered fifty years later lying on a sand dune on the North Island of New Zealand, a journey of some 10,000 miles. A message-containing barrel released by the American Admiral Melville near Cape Barrow in Alaska in September 1899, was recovered on the north coast of Iceland about six years later, having travelled at least 2,500 miles and being 'out' for 2,092 days.

At one time the Board of Admiralty ordered all HM ships to take part in bottle-post experiments, and the necessary printed paper was available for requisition through RN Stores. It was a common thing for bottle messages to request finders to pass details to Lloyds.

There have been many records of west-to-east journeys across the Atlantic in middle and higher latitudes, and east-to-west travels in low latitudes (see page 20). The eastward journey from New York waters to France and the Iberian Peninsula takes an average of 550 days.

Not all messages are of a scientific or navigational nature. In 1842 the brig *Superior*, an emigrant vessel commanded by Donald Mansen, was on passage from Thurso to Quebec. At the position 53° 48'N, 24°W she released the bottle-message 'This morning a male child was born; mother and infant are in a fair way and passengers are all in a healthy state'. In due course this bottle covered 1,500 sea miles and stranded on a beach within 2 miles of Thurso, the ship's departure point.

The cases where bottle-post has been used in real disaster are not so easy to track down, but no doubt they've occurred often enough. In July 1884, some fishermen picked up a distress message which seems likely to have been genuine. The bottle was found stranded in Morecambe Bay; the message stated that the crew of the vessel *Himalaya* saw death ahead of them. The ship's sails had been blown away; the propeller was broken; the hull was holed; she had been cast on the rocks near to Newfoundland, and Captain Roberts and his crew of sixteen were on the point of drowning. 'There is nothing we can do to save ourselves', read the message; 'if God does not intervene with a miracle we shall perish'. The note was signed by J. Roberts, the captain.

In 1949 a distress message which was certainly genuine was found in a bottle which had been released forty-five years earlier by the polar explorer Evelyn Baldwin. He had scribbled a hasty note calling for aid, had enclosed it in a small water-tight container, and cast it into the Arctic Ocean. The message drifted and remained undiscovered for nearly half a century until a Soviet fisherman discovered it in the sea ice in the Russian arctic. The note, written in Norwegian and English read: 'Five ponies and 150 dogs remaining. Desire hay, fish and 30 sledges. Must return early in August. Baldwin.' In fact, although the message arrived forty-five years too late, the expedition returned safely; Baldwin died a natural death at his home in 1933.

Bottle-post has been used by evangelists to carry the word; by

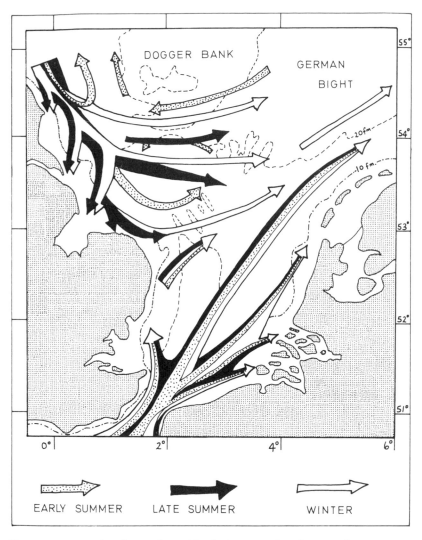

DOGGER BANK

GERMAN BIGHT

55°
54°
53°
52°
51°

0°   2°   4°   6°

EARLY SUMMER   LATE SUMMER   WINTER

Bottom currents in the southern North Sea, as plotted from the returns of Woodhead seabed drifters (after a chart in Laboratory Leaflet No 6, Fisheries Laboratory, Lowestoft).

distillers to promote their taste; and by broadcasters to publicise their products. A bottle was set adrift outside New York harbour by the sponsors of a radio programme with a note inside offering the reward of $1,000 to the finder. It was not a hoax and after a 2,500-mile passage the reward was successfully claimed by an Azorean boy. A bottle found in 1942 contained a message from the skipper of a launch which had been lost seven months earlier. It contained a will written on the back of a blank cheque. An American bachelor consigned to the sea fifteen copies of a proposal in fifteen sealed bottles. In due course he received four acceptances. Years ago the organisers of the Irish Sweepstake produced a bottle shaped like a fish, containing a leaflet with information and the Dublin address from which sweepstake tickets were available. The most attractive part of this scheme was a credit note good for £1 when presented to the landlord of the local inn.

Bottle-post is used today by the crews of tankers rounding the Cape of Good Hope. They consign their mail, with a little money, in bottles which regularly come ashore along the coast of Cape Province.

Drift bottles are, however, above all, a scientific proposition, and one of the most romantic of research techniques. So it is appropriate to leave them with a reference to Alfred de Vigny's poem 'La Bouteille à la Mer'. He relates that, in 1842, a bottle is thrown out in the open sea with a label 'catch me who can'. After many vicissitudes, it is retrieved by a young fisherman who straightway takes his precious find to a wise man, demanding to be told the nature of the elixir within it. The answer comes in ringing tones: 'Quel est cet elixir! Pêcheur, c'est la Science.'

So, in the interests of science, I want to put in a good word against the silly practice of sending false messages to sea in a bottle-boat. There are too many records of bottles which have been consigned to the sea carrying messages of non-existent distress and every kind of hoax. In the light of known existence of genuine emergency messages these are clearly only for the feeble-minded. The bare record of date and position confided to a bottle securely corked and sealed and ballasted to float with minimum freeboard, offers a prospect far more practical and exciting than jolly jokes about castaways on desert islands. But do not forget to include your name and address!

The currents which have been so effectively charted by drift devices over the years, eventually carry their flotsam to a beach, and the action of sea water on the beach itself is of absorbing interest. For the material of the beach, whether it is small particles of sand or large pebbles, is constantly on the move.

In mythology, Zeus or Neptune, the god of the sea, was also known as Earth-shaker, a much-deserved name. The pounding force of a wave on the beach may be as much as $6\frac{1}{2}$ tons per square foot. It is no wonder that the living creatures inhabiting these regions are specially designed to withstand pressure. In winter storms, granite blocks are torn from seaside promenades, and the sea hurls pebbles and boulders at the cliffs. We may call the seashore a battleground, but it is as well to concede that the sea is the greater force and that it calls the tune to which the land dances.

Waves are formed by wind pressure, which causes the sea to undulate into ridges of water—crests separated by troughs—which drive along at a slight angle from the direction of the wind. The stronger the wind, the greater the waves, but the size of them is affected very much by the 'fetch' of sea—the uninterrupted distance over which the wind has play. In sheltered waters a severe wind will only raise a short chop, whereas in open sea the same wind will produce violent effects.

In shallow waters, for instance, when a wave approaches the shore and is affected by friction with the sea bed, it changes its character, becoming shorter and with a steepening slope, until it eventually topples over. After breaking, it goes back to sea again, creating an undertow beneath the next advancing wave.

There is a scouring action along the shoreline, in which, generally speaking, the bigger the wave the greater the movement. Large waves tend to move the larger pebbles the greatest distance, small waves move the smaller particles. And it seems that for a particular size of wave there is a particular size of material which moves at the greatest rate. However, waves rarely hit a beach exactly square on, and their oblique arrival causes beach pebbles to be displaced either one way or the other along the beach. These findings were confirmed by research geologists who traced the movements of individual pebbles by marking them with marine paint and then following their progress day by day over a period of weeks. Other marking techniques include the use of radio-active isotopes, acoustic pebbles and fluorescent dyes.

So the character of the beach is shaped by the wind-formed waves which pound or play against it. The strength of the wind and the fetch determine the size of those waves. Even a gentle breeze may produce large waves provided the fetch covers hundreds or thousands of miles. A 10 knot breeze may produce 5ft waves and these waves may continue long after their formative wind has died; in these conditions we have what is called a groundswell. Now a submerged and unobstructed pebble of 5in diameter will be moved by water travelling at 2 knots. Smooth stones of 2–3in diameter may be shifted on a shingle beach by water travelling at 4 knots. If the pebbles are too large to move, then the sea batters at them till they become small enough. The motion of the sea tends to distribute the beach material in an even layer, and it constantly exerts a grading motion. Since it's easier to move downhill, there is a tendency for pebbles to move away offshore.

In a storm, the sea will pick up pebbles and stones and hurl them at the cliffs. Over a period of time, the cliffs are reduced to beach material, forming a ridge—a storm beach.

There are, of course, other forces at work, such as frost, sun and rain, and their effects are not confined to times of heavy weather. The coast has a lot to contend with, and the foreshore is indeed a restless and dynamic piece of country. But not only does it move; it lives!

2 The living beach

Life is never dull for a beach. At one moment it is covered by salt water; perhaps gently, perhaps pounding down with a force of several tons per square foot; at the next it is revealed to the atmosphere, which in turn may be hot and dry, then cold and wet with rain. No other kind of habitat is exposed to such a sequence of extreme conditions. So we may safely conclude that seashore plants are the tough nuts of the living world and the more we learn about them, the more wonderful they become. For they are not tough nuts in the crude sense. They are tough by virtue of painstaking adaptation. The seas may hurl themselves in fury, but the limpet presents the face which turneth away wrath; the periwinkles and whelks cluster in the shelter of a crevice and seaweeds rock and sway in tune with the swell, never fighting it.

Not all beaches are alive. Where the battle is greatest between sea and land, where cliffs are being slowly broken down, the shingle beaches are not congenial to plant or animal. The pebbles grind and crush against each other and very little can live in this heaving mass. It is only at the very top of the beach, where the tidal effect is least or non-existent, that plants may colonise and bind the stones to stop their fatal grinding.

When the pebbles have reached the end of their grinding days, however, and they have become grains of sand, a new stage begins. The sand grains are carried away by the action of wave and current and deposited in more sheltered areas. Places which are protected perhaps by a headland or spit. And there they build up into the sandy beaches which are beloved by children and adults and beach-combers alike.

The magical thing about those sand grains is that although they are individually so tough, and packed tightly against their neighbours, they are small enough to retain a coating of sea water around them by capillary action even during the period when the tide has retreated. This means that the sterile grinding action is so reduced that the beach is capable of supporting life. Above high-water mark, where the sand is dry, the rasping effect does occur and the habitat is correspondingly less fertile. Like the shingle beach, it is then only on the much higher level, where there is no wave action, that primitive plants can start their work of binding the dunes and making life possible for other species.

Down in the salt-wet sand there is a wealth of activity. Burrowing underneath the surface, a worm or a shellfish can retreat downwards if life gets uncomfortable on the surface—if it is too hot from the sun, too fresh from the rain or too mobile from pounding surf. When conditions are suitable, the worm can show his face and feed from the passing show of constantly renewed waterborne nutrients. In the right conditions there may be many millions of shellfish living within a single acre of tidal sand, feeding on the current-borne plants which flourish in the top layers of the sea. The phytoplankton blooms in the spring, as the days grow longer and there is increased light and radiation to stimulate them. Then in early summer they are at their most plentiful. A second harvest comes along in autumn, triggered by the availability of deep-water nutrients which have come to the surface. When the days get shorter there is a winter decline in sea-plant activity. So, although the sea and shore may appear unchanging to the casual observer, there is in fact a procession of seasons as we know it on land.

The plankton animals and plants, which are small but so numerous that they can support massive beasts like the basking shark, are the key to all the life of the shore. They provide the basic food, both for the fish and the crustaceans hunting in the shallow water, and for the shells and worms which sit tight waiting for their dinners to come to them.

Although many of the sandy-shore animals are themselves hidden out of sight, it is easy enough to trace them. Sand-masons, for instance, live in a tube which they make from grains of sand and shell particles and a mucus secretion (see page 37). The worm migrates up and down the tube according to tidal conditions. The top end reaches out above the surface of the beach so that the worm has access to the sea when the tide is in. Then its tentacles emerge and fan out and sweep the adjacent surface for food. The construction of the house is a very precise affair, the sand grains fitting to each other like a tubular jig-saw puzzle. Indeed the casing may well last longer than the worm. After a storm, you may find large numbers of the empty tubes thrown up on the strand line, but for live specimens look near low-water mark, around and about places which make a break in the beach—a groyne or a small weedy outcrop of rock.

The lugworm is the commonest sand worm. The familiar conical mound of castings is defaecated by the worm which lives in an L- or U-shaped burrow. Above its head is a tell-tale depression in the sand. This is caused by the caving-in of the sand as the worm eats away underneath. Unlike the sand-mason, the lugworm does not construct a permanent burrow although he strengthens his tunnel by lining it with mucus. He may live in one place for some weeks. He feeds by ingesting quantities of sand and then extracting the small portion which is edible. Periodically he backs up the burrow and adds to the mound of castings (pages 35 and 37). Lugworms are large, juicy beasts, very attractive to fish, and that is why you often see fishermen with fork and bucket digging away on the sand or mud collecting them for bait.

You may also see fishermen armed with buckets and short rakes. But these are not searching for bait, but directly engaged in fishing for marine molluscs. For lying just underneath the surface of the sand there will be a whole regiment of shellfish. In the case of cockles, the

Signs in the sand: herring gull and crab footprints, lugworm casts and craters.

numbers may be staggering. Marine biologists estimated that on one cockle bed in South Wales, covering an area of just over 300 acres, there were something like 462 million. The cockles live just below the surface, where they find some safety from predators. They are surprisingly mobile, with a strong muscular foot which they use to dig themselves in or jump about on the surface. A whole population of cockles may migrate if conditions change and better feeding is found elsewhere. They feed by siphoning in water from just above the sand-surface, sieving it through gills, and then ejecting it through a second siphon.

Cockles are an easy catch, but other burrowing bivalves are by no means easily collected. Some may burrow faster than you can dig. Razorshells (page 37) have a very powerful foot which pulls the smoothly designed shell vertically downwards. They do not only descend in the sand to avoid fishermen. In low-water conditions when a hot sun is drying the surface of the beach, they will need to get down into the damper, more sympathetic regions away from the danger of desiccation.

Unlike those worms which give clear surface signs of their underground occupation, the razorshells are not so easy to find. But as you walk along the tide line near low water, a sudden squirt of water and sand leads you to identify a shallow depression. Knowing the animal is there though is just the beginning of the battle, which has to be fought very quietly and gently. If you are going to dig the animal out then you have to move very fast, and unless you rapidly learn the trade it is fairer not to ply it, because on the occasions when you do bring up the razorshell, it is likely to be in two parts. A surer method, although it seems slightly unsporting, is to sow some salt in the centre of the depression. The sharply increased salinity is uncomfortable for the animal, which shows itself just above the surface. Even now, you must grip it firmly and extract it quickly, for the foot at the bottom-hinged-end of the shell is a powerful digging and pulling device. Having achieved a whole specimen, it is worth letting it go again just for the pleasure of watching the beautiful way in which it digs back to the safety of the sand.

The burrowing starfish, too, is quickly under the surface, digging

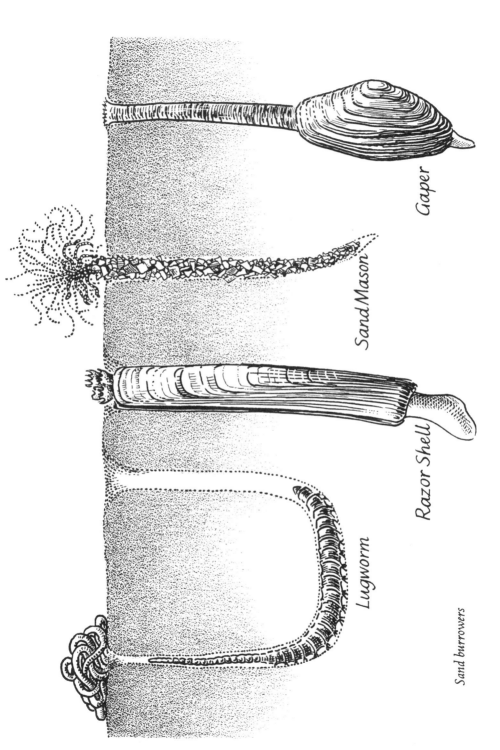

Gaper

Sand Mason

Razor Shell

Lugworm

Sand burrowers

with the many feet under the five arms. Safely out of sight, it will attack the molluscs and almost anything else which it encounters on its journey. Embracing perhaps a cockle, the suction of its feet forces the mollusc to open. Then the starfish extends its stomach through its mouth and presents it to the prey, devouring it at source. They are not loved by inshore fishermen, who say that if you have a starfish in the pot then there will not be any lobster. Before they realised the folly of it, fishermen used to deal with starfish by breaking them on the boat's gunwale and then tossing the pieces back to the sea. Since the starfishes' arms are capable of separate regeneration the result of this course of action was to increase the population of starfish. Starfish are regarded as a great pest on oyster and mussel beds. About the only good thing said for them is that they seem to prefer the slipper limpet as prey. And the slipper limpet competes with oysters for the same kind of food, and is therefore not popular among fishermen. But it has to be said that, on the whole, fishermen object to any competitor, and that this objection is not necessarily a justified one. The relationship between predator and prey is most often a mutually beneficial one.

Other starfish live above ground, for instance the brittle-stars, fragile and skinny versions of the plump common starfish. They live exposed on the surface, sometimes in unbelievable numbers. Estimating by photography, one biologist reckoned that a seething mass seen off Plymouth contained over a million to the acre, and the patches where they were seen might be several square miles in extent.

Sea potatoes, low-water creatures, burrow into sand and extend a lined tunnel up to the surface from which they siphon food. They can burrow out of sight in about 15 minutes. Incredibly, there is a Californian sea urchin which actually burrowed completely through steel piles $\frac{3}{8}$ in thick, by continually scraping them shiny and allowing the leaching sea water to take effect. Other rock-boring sea urchins in the Pacific make holes several inches deep, into which they wedge themselves in safety. Sea urchin eggs have yet another dubious claim to fame. The eggs have been rocketed into space as part of an experiment to test living organisms for the effects of cosmic rays.

Back on the beach again, where there are rocky outcrops or stony places, we will find another large group of animals which lives out in the open for all to see: marine snails, sea snails or gastropods. With few exceptions, they have a single spiral shell which, however, comes in many variations, some plain and dull, some very fancy and highly coloured.

The most easily seen are the limpets, with their flattened conical shells. Very often they live side by side with acorn barnacles (which are in fact crustaceans, cemented to the rock, and which, when covered by water, wave their legs about to collect the plankton). The limpets start life as free-swimming members of the plankton, but then settle on a patch of rock which they proceed to farm. They move about a given area, a couple of square yards, grazing off the algae. Usually they feed at night, some species returning to the same 'home'. If the rock is soft then over a period of time, because of erosion, the limpet

Dog whelks, acorn barnacles, limpets with channel wrack. Whelk-egg capsules above the right-hand bunch of weed.

will find himself returning to a well-marked depression. The low-profile shape of the shell offers least resistance to the force of the sea, and as you will know if you have given advance warning when trying to lift them, they have a foot muscle with a very strong grip. A cautious approach and a sharp thump usually catches them off their guard. Remember then that the kindly, if inquisitive, limpet-watcher puts the specimen back comfortably on his own home after inspection.

Both periwinkles and dog whelks are also common sea snails, to be found in profusion on and around rocky shores. They do not grip the rock surface with anything like the tenacity of the limpets, but find their safety from the force of the sea by retreating into crevices and crannies, or by hanging onto seaweed and bending to the ebb and flow. The periwinkles feed on algae and on lichens, and are very diverse in colour. Some are a beautiful yellow, others are green, brown, red or black. Sometimes they look rather like the bladders on some of the seaweeds, but they are certainly not in the least difficult to find.

The dog whelk is much more sinister. He is a carnivore and a predator, specially equipped for boring through the shells of other snails. When you consider that those others have developed techniques which defy the shattering force of the sea, clearly the dog whelk must have powerful weapons to defeat them. He has. He finds a suitable victim—limpet, top-shell or periwinkle perhaps—and he bores a hole through its shell, using teeth which he extends at the end of a proboscis. Having bored an entrance, the teeth cut out the meat from the prey, and convey it back to the throat of the whelk. However, the preferred prey species is either a barnacle or a mussel, because of course they cannot move off when attacked. When it has been feeding on mussels, the whelk shell itself changes colour to a browny-black or mauve-pink. In fact the whelk secretes a purple dye—purpurin—which was used by monks to illuminate their manuscripts and by Roman emperors to dye their togas. A toxic substance, it is yellow when first exuded, then green and finally purple, changes taking place through the action of the sun.

Unlike the bivalve molluscs, like cockles, which move about under and over the sand fairly freely, mussels are anchored by a 'byssus', a collection of tough threads. Rather like a boat moored 'all fours' in a mud berth, where it has lines running out to anchors at all four 'corners', the mussel is ready to withstand a current no matter which way it attacks. The shape of the shell itself is designed to present least resistance to the sea, facing into it from whichever direction it comes. Sometimes, though, mussels are congregated so thickly that they cannot move at all. Even if one is broken adrift it can very quickly send out new anchor cables and make itself fast again.

None of these animals could exist at all if it were not for the fact that the sea, in its tidal comings and goings, provides and sustains their necessary food. Food in the shape of water-borne plankton, and in the shape of intertidal algae. A sandy shore is not a very attractive habitat for plants. There are seaweeds in profusion on stones and rocks or anywhere where they can get a firm grip. But it is plain to see that holding fast to shifting sand is no joke, and on exposed beaches it is impossible.

Eel-grass, a flowering plant related to pond weed, is a pioneer which can establish itself in relatively sheltered sand, provided there is a substratum of muddiness in which it can entrench its roots. An undistinguished-looking, grass-like plant, it nevertheless supports its own community of life, and it is a great pity that not only has it been much reduced by disease, but that it has a genius for growing in those areas which are attractive to large-scale 'developers'. Eel-grass is the preferred food of the brent goose, and large numbers of these splendid birds migrate from the Arctic breeding grounds to the sand flats at Foulness. There are now not enough places around the coasts of Europe where they may find food, and the long-term outlook for brents must be poor. Another, much smaller, but no less important, patch of eel-grass is on the Exe estuary in Devon, but here there is talk of a new yacht marina. The submarine grass could hardly be called a spectacular sight, yet it supports a curious group of animals, including snails and sea hares, cuttle fish and pipe fish, quite apart from the brent geese. From the point of view of vegetation, though, sandy shores are something of a marine desert, and it is not until you are well above high-water mark, where sand movement is reduced, that some tough pioneering plants, resistant to wind, salt spray and drought,

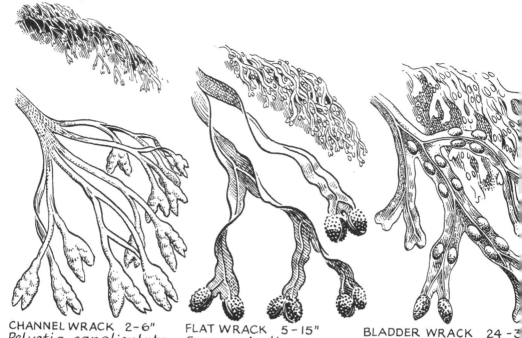

CHANNEL WRACK 2-6"
Pelvetia canaliculata

FLAT WRACK 5-15"
Fucus spiralis

BLADDER WRACK 24-3
Fucus vesiculosus

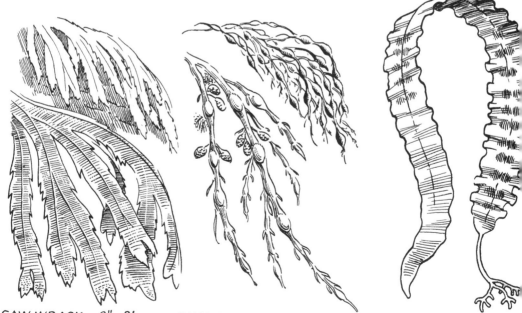

SAW WRACK 8"-2'
Fucus serratus

KNOTTED WRACK 15"-5'
Ascophyllum nodosum

SUGARY WRACK 8"-8'
Laminaria saccharina

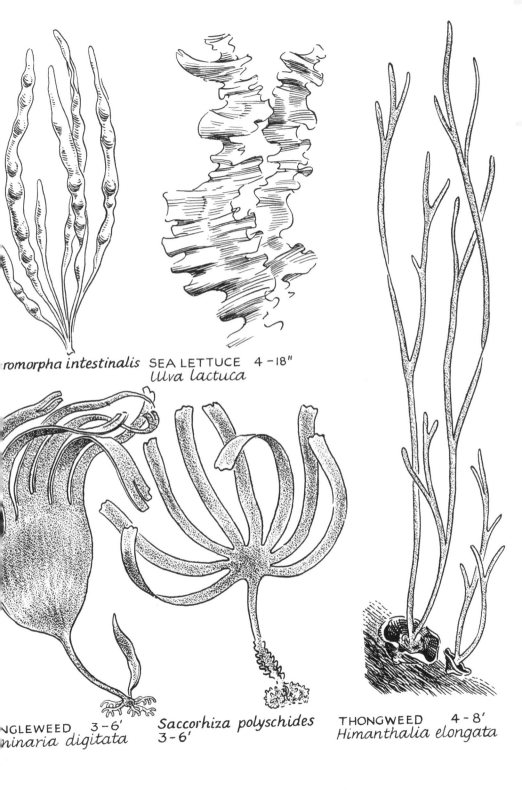

romorpha intestinalis SEA LETTUCE 4-18"
Ulva lactuca

NGLEWEED   3-6'   *Saccorhiza polyschides*   THONGWEED   4-8'
ninaria digitata   3-6'   *Himanthalia elongata*

can penetrate deep down to set up a root system which begins the process of stabilisation.

But whenever there is an outcrop of rock or stones, then there will be a rich and varied display of seaweeds in the intertidal area. Seaweeds are broadly classified in four groups by colour: blue-green, brown, green and red. Some are very large and tough, some are fragile and diaphanous, and they represent a largely untapped potential for food and commercial purposes. For many hundreds of years seaweed has been utilised on a small scale, and it seems likely that sooner or later someone will overcome the difficult problems of successfully farming this huge natural resource.

One of the widely-used species is Irish moss, or carragheen, an edible seaweed once thought to have important medicinal properties. Washed and boiled, it was infused as a beverage, or concentrated to make table jellies, after the addition of sugar and fruit juice. Dulse has been eaten in quantity in Ireland and Scotland, where the cry of 'dulse and tangle' used to be heard in the streets. One of the commonest of red seaweeds, it grows from disc-shaped holdfasts fixed to large brown seaweeds. It may be chewed fresh or dried, or boiled in milk. It has even been used as a substitute for chewing tobacco.

On North Ronaldshay, the northernmost island of Orkney, there is a breed of small short-tailed sheep which graze on *Laminaria* and *Ascophyllum*. These brown seaweeds—tangleweeds and wracks—are good food, comparable in nutritional value with meadow hay. The resulting meat is dark and rich.

For many years seaweeds have been used as food for man and beast, and for manure. The brown, intertidal species are used for manure, either fresh or in rotting piles. It is a common sight to see enthusiastic gardeners loading up their car boots with storm-piles of rotting tangleweed, rich in potash and moisture-conserving. On a larger scale, farmers collect seaweed piles and spread it on the fields. In Ayrshire, seaweed has been spread on potato fields at the rate of 30 tons per acre. In the Isles of Scilly, my good friend Bernard Bond, who is alas no longer with us, used to take horse and cart down to the sand flats after a storm, and we would bring it back loaded to the gunwales with the sweet-smelling sea-hay.

Farmers take advantage of storm-wrecked seaweed, rich in potash, for fertiliser. Mount's Bay, Cornwall.

A factory for the production of seaweed manure was built in the United States as long ago as 1870, and commercial companies are still marketing sophisticated liquid versions. Recent research has shown that seaweed products increase the uptake of plant nutrients, impart a degree of frost resistance, and make plants better able to withstand the attack of certain fungus and insect pests. Claims that had been considered extravagant were in fact substantiated. It seems likely that there is going to be a considerable growth in the seaweed industry as soon as factory methods can be developed to culture algae as a source of protein.

In the old days, collecting *Laminaria* and *Fucus* (variously known as kelp, oarweed and tangleweed) and manufacturing kelp was a major industry in some remote islands. In Orkney, for instance, 20,000 men were employed for the whole of the summer. The weed was collected, dried in the sun and then burnt in shallow pits. While the mass was still hot it was sprinkled with water to break it up. From about 20 tons of the wet weed the result was about one ton of hard dark grey ash. Sodium carbonate and potash were subsequently extracted. The soda was used in the manufacture of glass and soap, while the potash was sold as fertiliser.

The British kelp industry went into a decline after the Napoleonic wars, when the ash was more cheaply imported from France, but it revived after the discovery of iodine in 1811. For a long time kelp was the only source, although the preparation was fraught with difficulties. If the untreated weed was washed by rain, for instance, nearly 90 per cent of the iodine was lost.

If you are collecting seaweed for your garden, the best time to do it is after a summer storm, when great quantities of rich kelp will have been torn from its anchorage and piled up on the shore. Transport it and use it before rain reduces its value.

The fronds and holdfasts of weed provide food and shelter for many animals. Just take a close look at any of the brown seaweed fronds and there may be the characteristic rasp marks showing where limpets have fed. There will probably be periwinkles feeding, and perhaps the very small, but delicately patterned blue-rayed limpet nestling in the depression it has eaten away. There may be the almost fluorescent mossy mats made by communities of Bryozoa—sea mats—each minute compartment occupied by an animal which extends

Cut-away view of dogfish eggcase and yolk sac. (Woodcut from Yarrell's British Fishes, 1836.)

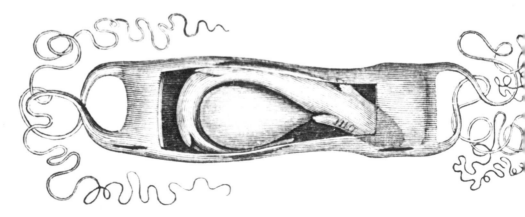

Cluster of dogfish egg purses

feeding tentacles to the plankton. Polychaete worms live in limey tubes which spiral and snake about on the weed surface.

Attached to the weed may be the small egg capsules of sea slugs and snails, the purses of netted whelk, ribbons of sea lemon, strings of sea hare and collar of necklace shell. At extreme low-water mark of the bigger spring tides, you may find the elegant creamy purses of the dogfish egg, lashed to the kelp by twisty threads (see page 47). They are easy enough to find if they are there at all. The embryo must incubate for about six months in this egg case before it splits open and the young fish emerges into the sea. The other 'mermaid's purses' may also be found lashed to weeds at low-water mark. These are the darker eggs of skates and rays, all containing the young fish and his supply of yolk.

The small animals which breed so plentifully on seaweed and along the seashore are a great attraction for birds, some of which are highly specialised beach-feeders. Turnstones are very typical shore waders, with their mottled tortoiseshell upper parts, short orange legs and short pointed bill. They are very tame and so wonderfully camouflaged that very often you nearly stumble over them before they take off with shrill cries, flying low over the water, showing a bold pied pattern. They almost always land again after a short flight so that you get a chance to see them at work. In small parties they delve among the weed and stones and debris, jerking it about and turning things over in the search for molluscs, insects and sand-hoppers. They are, in short, on the same job as you; they are honest beachcombers.

Very often the parties of turnstones are accompanied by a small party of purple sandpipers. Rather portly birds, confiding and tame, easily missed but especially fond of rocky places, weedy shores, weedy and encrusted piers and suchlike man-made structures, dodging the sea and chasing small morsels. Sanderlings are also very adept shore hunters; another plump wader, pale chestnut and white, not so much noticeable for their colour as for their extraordinary vitality. They scream along the edge of the surf like clockwork mice, snatching unfortunate bugs and worms from the very edge of the surf and the backwash.

Oystercatchers, unlike the smaller camouflaged waders, are only too easily seen and heard, with their pied plumage, long orange bills, and high-pitched peeping. They congregate on low-water sand flats, probing for cockles and worms, and after they have flown away you will find the impressions of their bills deep down in the sand. They have very powerful bills, adapted for the job of opening cockles, crabs and limpets.

Cockles they deal with very easily, as the shell is broken with a few hammer blows, but a mussel takes more expertise. The bird turns it upside down so that its flat surface is exposed. Then it hammers away at this vulnerable part. Once a hole has been made, the oystercatcher's bill probes inside, prises the valves apart and

Sanderlings

Oystercatcher
digging for cockles

Herring
Gull

Turnstones

Ringed Plovers

Common Tern

achieves the flesh. His technique with a limpet is to approach quietly and then give a short but powerful sideways blow. In shallow water he will stalk his prey in the hope of finding a bivalve shell open and feeding. In this case, one sharp blow of that hefty beak will pierce in and cut the adductor muscle, thus relaxing the shell.

But the oystercatcher has to keep a sharp eye open for herring gulls, for very often they will wait for the moment of triumph and then dash in and steal the food from the rightful owner. Herring gulls are the scavengers of the shore, doing a useful job of clearing up the debris and rotting tide-line corpses, but they are not above eating a fresh mollusc. In fact it is very difficult to find anything that a gull will not eat.

It is fashionable in seaside towns to decry sea gulls as noisy and dirty beasts, mainly because of their unfortunate habit of leaving nitrogen-rich deposits on lovingly-polished motor cars. But as members of a very successful species, herring gulls are interesting creatures. I admire the logical way in which they have taken to nesting alongside

Turnstones, sanderlings and dunlin waiting for the tide to fall and uncover the beach feeding grounds.

the warm chimney tops of fishing ports, or towns with a large population of retired people; both places provide them with a never-failing
source of easy food and it is good sense to live close to the dining
room. They do a useful job, quite apart from their seashore patrolling
work, by frequenting rubbish tips and cleaning up the decaying food
items which would be only too promptly colonised by flies. Gulls
have some clever techniques of their own for dealing with shellfish
and worms. Having found a mollusc, they will fly up high above a
pavement or concrete hard and drop it until it cracks open. Or, on a
watery meadow or puddly beach they will stamp their feet up and
down in such a manner as to compress the sand and encourage the
worm to show his face—for the last time. And you may see them
quartering the marshes like a harrier for small mammals or plunging
under water to catch crabs. All in all they are clever beasts, but there
is no doubt they have increased in numbers at an alarming rate, and
that they have the distressing—to us—habit of eating other birds'
eggs and young when they get the chance.

Several species of gull spend their time on the coast, and most of
them nest nearby. But the black-headed gull, the one with the red
legs and beak and a black head (at least in summer; during winter it
has a black eye-stripe) often breeds on inland sites, on the borders of
fresh water far from the sea. One species, the gentle kittiwake, is less
piratical than the others and is largely ocean-going outside the breeding season.

Occasionally you will see the graceful sea-swallows, the terns,
hovering and plunge diving for fish at the edge of the sea. These
birds are one of the few which actually nest on the beach, although
the construction is hardly worthy of the name. They choose a slight
depression on a shingle bank or sand dune or rocky islet, then lay
about three eggs which effectively merge into their surroundings so
that they are most difficult to find. Most species of tern nest gre-
gariously in well-established colonies. Sadly, human pressures often
make life impossible for them, since they are not the only ones to
enjoy living on the top of the beach overlooking the sea.

Ringed plovers, too, suffer from having a habitat preference which
coincides with the picnic family. Although they start nesting as early

as March they tend to go on raising repeat families even into August. Typically they choose sandy or shingly sea beaches, quite close to the extreme high-water mark, sometimes even along the strandline. Again the nest is not much more than a scrape, perhaps lined with a few shells, grass or odd bits of litter. Unless you watch the bird returning to its eggs it is most difficult to find.

In rabbit burrows among the sand dunes, under furze or bramble bushes, sometimes under rocks, the shelduck nests. A fine big duck with bold plumage—black and white with a chestnut breast-band and a bright red bill and pink feet—it is not an animal you could miss. In addition to this it is a sociable creature which very often gathers together in flocks numbering hundreds. It feeds on molluscs and crustacea, small fish and worms, which it collects by wading or by actively sweeping across mud. One of its favourite foods is a little snail, *Hydrobia ulvae*, which occurs in truly remarkable numbers—over 40,000 on one square yard of mud! Shelducklings face many hazards in their first few weeks of life, but, unlike the estuary breeders, those which choose to nest on the sea coast very often get drowned in the pounding surf. They are very often 'rescued' by well-meaning people who see them come ashore exhausted and, having frightened the parent birds away feel responsible for the ducklings which, in fact, only need a rest and a bit of peace.

Many other birds visit the beach irregularly for food. Garden birds like robins and dunnocks, pied wagtails and pigeons will all take advantage of strand line feeding if they happen to live nearby. If you extend your interest to the sea cliffs then a whole new range of species comes into focus. On remote western coasts, choughs may nest in a cliff crevice almost within reaching distance from beach level. Rock doves breed in sea caves, but they are pretty rare birds now, and almost hopelessly degenerated by intermixing with other pigeons to form the well-known London street pigeon, the feral pigeon. But the pure rock dove is a genuine coastal bird, living on wild coast and building crevice nests. Thousands of years ago they were first domesticated by people who encouraged them to breed on convenient man-made ledges. Convenient for the farmer, that is, so that he was able to take the squab when it had reached the right stage of fatness. These cave-bred rock doves almost certainly were the fore-runners of the dove-cote pigeon, which was bred in enormous numbers until as late as the eighteenth century in times when fresh meat was scarce in winter. (Pigeons obligingly breed more-or-less throughout the year.)

Another bird which breeds in a hole or recess in the cliff is the rock pipit, very much a coastal species which haunts the tide line and spray-splashed rocks for crustaceans and vegetable titbits. Rather a drab-looking little bird, you are most likely to have your attention drawn to it by its metallic call 'tsup, tsup'. Shags, too, nest in rock crevices, building a great bulky edifice of sticks. The nest and its surroundings soon become attractively white, at least attractive until you approach closely and smell!

Higher up the cliff kittiwakes, guillemots, razorbills, fulmars and herring gulls all find their homes, each having a slightly different requirement so that although they all live in close proximity they do not encroach on each other's preferred territory. Jackdaws, ravens and buzzards often breed on cliff faces, but the king of them all is the peregrine, a falcon with swift flight, pouncing on a pigeon or seabird with a splendid headlong swoop. After a catastrophic decline in population almost certainly caused by misuse of agricultural chemicals, the species may now be recovering. Although individual pigeons and auks may not be cheered at the news, it is to be hoped that in the interests of healthy diversity of species this falcon will succeed.

Mammals are not uncommon along the seashore. Apart from you and me, foxes regularly patrol beaches and strand lines looking for carrion and for rabbits, which graze and nibble at the vegetation at the top of the beach. Otters often leave their foot prints as proof that they sometimes do some sea-fishing, but you would be very lucky to see one.

The most typical seashore mammal is the seal. Grey seals tend to prefer remote west coast and Scottish beaches with sea caves and forbidding cliffs to protect them. Common seals, while overlapping in distribution with the grey in Scotland, tend to go for tidal sand-islands off the east coast. Both are highly attractive animals, but neither of them really welcomes human interference in spite of the fact that most of us are so well disposed towards them.

Common seal pup. They are not infrequently washed ashore undernourished and in need of help, but fat ones are only looking for a rest.

They have a fairly comfortable life, with the sea full of fish close at hand, and a gregarious beachful of their fellows for company. Common seals breed in mid-summer, dropping their pups on tidal sand banks from which they very soon have to learn to swim. Grey seals drop their pups well above high-water mark in caves or at the back of a beach, and the young seal normally lives ashore until he is a month old. Fed with very rich milk by his mother, he grows from a skinny white-coated thing to a barrel-shaped grey-coated moulter in the space of twenty-one days. At this point the mother abandons him for good. And when he is hungry he finds his own way to the sea, and food. In his first year he may wander, travelling as far as France or

Norway, but in due course he returns home to a quiet and sedentary life.

It is in their first few weeks at sea, in early winter, that young seals very often encounter storms and come ashore exhausted. Like those young shelducklings, it is in this condition that well-meaning rescuers either take the animals home with them, or try to launch them into the sea again, believing mistakenly that they cannot survive out of water. All they need is a little peace and quiet so that they can revive. Then, when the time is ripe, they will go off again.

These babies, which are invariably described in press reports as abandoned, are only rarely in need of food. If you have reason to believe that the seal is in genuine distress, then it can be fed either by stomach tube or by force feeding raw fish. If it is new-born or only a few days old, still in its white coat, then use a liquid mixture of 50 per cent agricultural fish meal and 50 per cent baby milk, with added

Grey seal pup. Abandoned by their mothers at three weeks old, seals go to sea to make a living. They too may be stormbound on beaches. Do not return them to the sea; they know the way.

cod liver oil. Ease a greased tube down through its mouth and into its stomach. Attach a funnel to the top and pour a pint or so of the mixture in in one fell swoop. The youngster can take more than you expect, and three times a day. If it is lively enough to bite and plunge about, you will need an assistant to straddle the animal and hold its mouth open with heavy gloves. If it is this lively then it can digest raw fish, which you will probably have to force down its throat with a stick. But please remember that the *likely* thing is that the seal is looking only for a rest, and get qualified advice if you possibly can. A sick or injured seal should, of course, be attended by a veterinary surgeon. And it is your job to pay the bill!

The other mammals which you may see from the beach are porpoises, dolphins and whales. On occasion quite large numbers of porpoises and dolphins may come close inshore to take advantage of a shoal of mackerel or mullet. Mostly all you will see is the dorsal fin rolling over and reappearing in slow rhythm. Very occasionally one of them may leap right out into the open and hang suspended before falling back with a mighty splash. Killer whales and pilot whales are sometimes seen round our coasts, but on the whole the chance of seeing them is small, and the chance of being eaten by one is even smaller.

The largest animal you are likely to see off the beach is the second biggest fish in the world, the basking shark. Reaching as much as 20 ft long, they cruise slowly along, just under the surface and sometimes very close inshore, with their wide-open mouths gulping in the plankton. They are easily distinguished from the whales by the fact that the large dorsal fin and tail fin are showing above water most of the time, whereas the whales' fins appear and disappear regularly in time with their breathing pattern. The great fish has no need to come to the surface to breathe, of course, and he just continues to suck up plankton in a phlegmatic manner. Although the appearance of a basking shark is guaranteed to clear the sea of bathers, the fact is that they are quite harmless. The only danger is that if you swim too close he may panic and, in diving, scrape your skin off with his sharkskin or knock you out with his flailing tail.

Harmless they may be, like most sharks, but like the wolf and the fox, they bear the wrong name and have to carry the can for centuries of ignorant character-blacking. Fortunately for them, the baskers are plankton feeders and will not take bait, or they would doubtless become the quarry of the sport fishermen, and yet another virility symbol would be born. Other sharks, being honest predators, are more vulnerable. Even in this enlightened age, people become heroes by virtue of catching a shark, a feat requiring no skill but a strong stomach and a certain amount of brute force. We even see boats flying special pennants and carrying grown men and women proud of belonging to a shark angling club, proof to the lesser mortals around them that they have conquered the pathetic, harmless, usually female but fiercely named shark.

Baskers appear off the west coasts of Scotland and Ireland in April/ May and off the south-west around about June, when they are in evidence for only a few weeks. At one time they were hunted for their valuable liver oil, a fairly dangerous occupation but, by contrast with the sport fishermens', an honourably motivated one. Nowadays they are mostly left alone on their majestic cruise of the shoreline. Great beasts and lowly ones alike, they live in the most fascinating of all worlds, and it is a joy to be part of it all as one of their fellows.

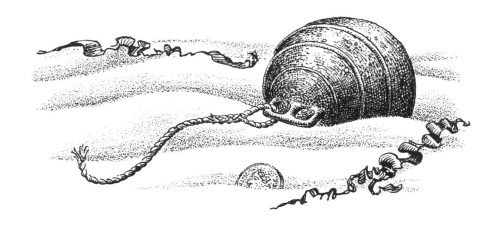

3 The gentle art of wrecking

Talk about 'wrecking' and most people see a vision of swarthy long-shoremen setting up false lights on the top of a cliff in dark and stormy weather, and luring innocent sailormen to an untimely death on the cruel shore. Never was a reputation so richly undeserved. It is not necessary here to relate how coastal people have risked their lives on untold occasions in order to rescue ships and sailors in distress. However one may deplore it, the fact is that ships do founder, and their cargoes are very often cast ashore. Wreck of varying kinds finds its way ashore from many different sources, and what law-abiding citizen can restrain his natural curiosity? What more natural than that he should investigate the unexpected windfall? On behalf of the Crown, whose foreshore he jealously and protectively patrols, the honest beachcomber does his duty and reports his findings to the Receiver of Wreck. About the activities of the less honest beach-comber we draw a discreet veil, but it is only proper, in defending the good name of wrecking, to make it abundantly clear that the activity involves only what the uninitiated calls beachcombing, no more no less. In the West Country, and perhaps elsewhere, no local ever speaks of going beachcombing, he goes wrecking; and if he's lucky he comes home with some wreck—a few nice pieces of timber and maybe a trawl float, or even a bottle with a message in it. He does not encourage ships to destruction. Neither, in truth, does he very often acquaint the Receiver of Wreck with his discoveries. But then, no right-minded Receiver would really want a procession of longshore vagabonds (dictionary definition of a beachcomber) laying choice pieces of gribbled planking and trawl floats on his desk. While it is true that, inside territorial waters, all wreck is the property of the Crown, it is not too difficult in practice to draw the line between what ought to be reported and what is better quietly tidied away.

Wrecking requires careful preparation. You are not going to wear your Sunday suit or your best shoes. Clearly you will wear old clothes and gumboots or canvas shoes. Remember that if you get them wet with salt-spray, or if you get boots full of sea, they must be washed in fresh water before they will dry properly. For when the sea water dries or evaporates it leaves salt behind, and since the salt is hygroscopic it will always attract moisture from the air. Lovely though it is to walk on the beach with bare feet, and bare everything else for that matter, it is dangerous because of broken glass, not to mention other horrors with which we will deal later. You should carry a pocket knife, a six-foot length of terylene cord for tying bundles of this and that, and a couple of plastic bags for specimens. You should know the times of high or low water and the likely trend of the weather. If you have human competition, then you may have to get up at crack of dawn to be first on the scene.

Some forms of wreck are not so attractive. These are the piles of household rubbish and municipal junk which sometimes get heaved over a cliff to rest in a cove for ages awaiting an extra high tide and storm to wash them away and redistribute them elsewhere. But it can be quite rewarding to search about under jetties and piers or public places where people may have thrown such things as bottles. Ginger beer and pop bottles may date back as far as the middle of the eighteenth century. These are likely to have an almost pointed bottom end, something of a bomb shape. They were eventually

Gale-force wind blowing onshore. Herring gulls do well feeding in the troughs. Next day the beach was strewn with hundreds of tellins, and beach-cocklers were hard at work.

patented in 1814 by William Hamilton and were popularly known as Hamiltons, or bowlers since they were unable to stand up unaided. Later designs introduced a flat bottom and involved a sort of double pinch in the neck, housing a glass marble which, under pressure, sealed the bottle—until it was forced down releasing pressure and allowing the contents to be drunk. Versions of these bottles, and the stone ginger-beer bottles which usually have a local legend stamped on them, were in common use until the 1940s. Very often you will find that the patent neck has been broken and schoolboys have re-cycled the glass marble.

You are unlikely to find a pop bottle with its load of pop intact, as they were notoriously unstable and liable to explode, and I suppose the chance of a 'whisky galore' is also slim. But barrels of spirits and wine not infrequently get washed ashore. Mr Williams, the Fisheries Officer at Plymouth, well remembers that during the World War II a whole lot of barrels came ashore at Mullion Cove. One was found to contain rum, and this started an avalanche of rescuers combing the beaches. Others contained a very rough red wine. In the 'A hundred years ago' column of the *Western Morning News* a short time ago there was a note about a butt of Tarragona wine which had been washed ashore near Sidmouth in Devon. What a delightful find. Nowadays we need to examine all barrels and canisters with a great deal more caution and less happy anticipation, because ships' cargoes tend to be more fearful than drinkable. Crude oil is one of the least worrying items when regular cargoes of things like toxic gases and agricultural chemicals trundle up and down the channel. If you do come across a suspicious canister or war-like object, then you should take careful notes of the inscription and inform the nearest coastguard (see telephone directory).

For wrecking you need a sharp eye. The general technique is obvious enough. Get the light behind you and walk along the strandline, not too fast. Keep your eyes firmly on the strandline, and yet take a long-shot of the distant view occasionally. Especially if there is any opposition, in the form of other wreckers, you must be careful not to miss the big stuff by looking too closely for the small. Sometimes you may have to walk fast slowly to get something someone else is closer to but has not yet seen. But no such technique will find you your basic treasure—coins. On popular beaches there will be favourite places where families spend the day. Invariably and regrettably, some coins fall out of trouser pockets and lose themselves just under the surface. Gently raking the sand in these places produces quick and substantial results. One almost professional coin collector in Dorset reckoned to make as much as £40 in three months using this technique, but she must know her patch very well. On any summer day in St Ives, you may see old men walking slowly across the beach pushing a stick and watching for coins in the furrow.

Succeeding tides may uncover and reveal coins lower down the beach, and if you choose the right place you may be rewarded with gold, or with a genuine Spanish piece-of-eight. One of my friends has some lovely silver coins washed ashore over a period of years from an Armada wreck off the south Devon coast.

The up-to-date method of coin searching is to use a metal detector, 'rugged, lightweight and transistorised' as they say. The advertising is very beguiling: 'locates bags of coins, pistols and knives up to three feet; and detects larger objects such as a metal chest as deep as five feet'. Who could resist it?

But there are other precious objects to be found apart from doubloons. In South Africa they actually find diamonds along the beaches of the south west. Ostriches have the habit of picking up hard stones to use as grinding devices in their gizzards. Naturally enough they prefer diamonds because they offer greatest hardness for a given size. At one time they were in real danger because diamond-hunters would shoot the ostriches in order to examine the gizzard for diamonds. Beach diamond hunting is now a strictly controlled commercial undertaking on a very grand scale. The beach sands are bulldozed and the diamond-bearing gravel screened out and millions of pounds worth of diamonds recovered from this richest deposit in the world.

European coasts cannot compete in the diamond stakes, but there are many semi-precious and ancient things to be found. Coal, for instance, may not have quite the glamour of a diamond, but at least it keeps you warm. Along the shores of the north east, coal waste that has been tipped onto the shore may be collected in hard times by diligent scavengers. In other parts of the country, in the past, poor people have collected the age-old peat and timber from submerged forests, after digging several feet through the sand or taking advantage of a storm which reveals the ancient fuel. Coal represents the fossilised remains of primitive vegetation from the marsh deltas of hundreds of millions of years ago; diamonds have the same origin.

On the Yorkshire coasts there is a deposit of carbonaceous shale which yields small lumps of a pure coal called jet. A semi-precious material, once highly prized for jewellery, it has been used by craftsmen since the Bronze Age. It dates from about 170 million years ago

The world's richest deposit of diamonds . . . beachcombing on the grand scale in South West Africa.

and is the fossilised version of a tree related to our monkey puzzle. Easily carved, it gives off an aromatic odour. Warm to the touch, and a bad conductor of heat, it generates a charge of static electricity when rubbed on fabric.

Perhaps the hey-day of jet jewellery was after the death of Prince Albert, when demand was great and the men of Whitby scoured the beaches after every tide to keep the craftsmen busy. Whitby was the recognised centre for the industry, although jet was found as far away as Kent, carried south by currents.

The raw jet is black only after it has been polished, or broken. The sea-washed pebbles look dull grey and scratchy. The procedure for identifying it is to rub the suspected pebble with emery paper—if brown scratch-lines appear, then it is jet. Nowadays there is no great demand for the material in Britain, although a few Whitby craftsmen still remain, but it is still worked on the Continent and in the USA.

Another very beautiful semi-precious stone which may be current-borne to us from the lignite beds of the Baltic, is amber. A fossil resin, some 40 million years old, it comes from the remains of coniferous trees of the oligocene epoch. The most important amber-producing region is East Prussia, and I well remember the pleasure of finding a fine piece the size of a pigeon's egg in a shop in Warsaw a year or so ago. It is systematically mined on the coast of Danzig. Like jet, it generates static electricity when rubbed against soft cloth, and in fact the Greeks, who first discovered the phenomenon, called it *electron*. Rough amber beads were worn in prehistoric times, and many primitive beliefs attach to it. In Britain, it was believed to prevent croup as late as the nineteenth century. It is found on the shores of the east coast, mostly in Norfolk and Suffolk, where it is nearly always tangled with seaweed and only too easy to miss. Amber comes in two forms, cloudy and an almost clear 'ice colour'. The clouded variety contains water droplets which have dried out, leaving behind their impression. The clearer version is probably formed by bleaching.

The only connection between amber and ambergris is in the name, for ambergris is a very different substance indeed, with no relation to

64

Anything from a tropical bean to a grand piano . . .

the fossilised resins and carbons. Sadly, your chance of finding any is very remote, unless you are sailing the China Seas, Indian Ocean or the tropical Atlantic. In fact, the penalties for finding it, and keeping it, can be severe. In the Maldive Islands all ambergris belongs to the Sultan, and you conceal it at risk of decapitation.

Ambergris is a secretion from the intestines of sperm whales, a product which may perhaps be compared with the intestinal stones or hair balls which occur in domestic cows and in other smaller whales. It is a pliable wax-like substance, brown or yellowy grey; it smells musky and is highly soluble in organic solvents. Using it as a fixative, scents retain their odour for months, so it is not surprising that it had great value, although the market has now passed its peak. In the Orient, it was prized as a powerful aphrodisiac, so its use in the expensive perfumes of today is logical enough.

A piece of ambergris weighing 44lb was sold in London for £2,018 in 1924, incidentally turning the Harris Whaling & Fishing Co Ltd's trading account to a profit in what had been a bad year! In 1953 the whaling scientist Robert Clarke was on board *Southern Harvester* when they removed a piece of ambergris weighing 918lb from the gut of a sperm whale, but even this was surpassed by a vessel of the Dutch East Indies Company which found one weighing 975lb. No wonder it is every beachcomber's dream to find some, when it is still so valuable. But beware of the many imitations. Paraffin wax, gastropod spawn and decomposed soapstone are all traps for the unwary.

One last word about precious stones. In both the oyster and the ormer there is the slight chance of finding a pearl. In the Channel Islands, where the ormer, a succulent Mediterranean species of limpet is very common, I was once shown a small palmful of little pearls which a local fishmonger had painstakingly collected. I hardly imagine that they have much market value, but they were very attractive and made a unique souvenir.

At one time pearls were thought to contain powerful medicinal properties. Dissolved in lemon juice or mixed with milk they were believed to cure stomach ulcers, improve your speaking voice and preserve chastity.

On the other hand, cowrie shells were more closely connected with conception and birth. With their superficial resemblance to the vulva, they have been much used in the form of amulets, guaranteed to guard against sterility and encourage children. Again, with a resemblance to a human eye, they were worn to give protection against the evil eye. Quite apart from their visual suitability, they lend themselves easily to necklace making since they are easy to bore and often come ashore with convenient holes broken in them already.

Cowries used to circulate as currency in parts of Africa, and even today the children of the Isles of Scilly call them 'moneypennies'. European cowries are rather small by tropical standards, but have the same shape and attractive characteristics. There are only two species found round our shores, both about half an inch long with 20–25 ribs. Feeding on sea-squirts, they live under rocks at extreme low water. The European cowrie has three brownish-purple spots and the Arctic cowrie is spotless. Both are common round our shores, though the European is rather more so than the Arctic.

In their stranded shell-only form, they are rather difficult to find, being well camouflaged among the beach debris. But on a suitable beach, like that on Tresco in the Scillies, or Bantham in Devon, you may find a good number. As an exercise, once, I spent twenty minutes concentrating on the job, and found 61 on the shell beach at Bantham; 35 were European and 26 Arctic cowries.

Cowrie shells bring a breath of the tropics to our beaches. Better (since they at least are honest citizens of Britain), than the dismal trade in tropical cowries and murex and cone shells which fill seaside souvenir shops in the summer. Fantastic shapes and beautiful colours they may have, but the trade is vile; the unfortunate inhabitant of the shell is boiled out just to provide a cheap and inappropriate souvenir.

I know that, to a serious collector, the only shell worth talking about is one that has been taken off the back of its live owner, but for most of us I like to think that the slightly battered and sun-bleached version thrown up on the beach is just as interesting. Often the 'lantern'—a helical whorl—is all that is left of a whelk shell on the

John Goddard and wreck-pile. No self-respecting fisherman-farmer in the Isles of Scilly lacks a stockpile like this one.

strandline, and a very intriguing and shapely thing it is, too. Often a shell will bear the signs of the animal which killed its occupant. A neatly bored round hole indicates that the carnivorous dog whelk has done his dirty work. And there may be the tube cases of bristle worms, limy scribblings and spiralling. One shell may have other shells and acorn barnacles clinging to it, forming a block of flats, and in rock pools it may have been taken over by a new inmate, the hermit crab.

Beach pebbles are worth examining closely, since they come in such a wide variety of colours and shapes. Few people can resist collecting the more attractive ones, but it is not so easy to know how to make use of them (apart from the pleasure of chucking them into the sea, one of the least harmful ways known to man of sublimating his aggressive instincts on difficult days!) You can invest in a 'tumble polisher', which, over a period of time, transforms the rough pebble surface into a gem. Mount it, thread a length of leather thong, and—instant hippy. There is quite a thriving business in this sort of thing in the Westcountry; Kernowcraft of 44 Lemon Street, Truro, Cornwall, have an excellent free catalogue if it interests you.

Sand-polished pieces of glass floats, pop and wine bottles, can look very attractive if they are piled into an old decanter or flagon, covered with water and placed on a windowsill where the sun may shine through them. One of those old fashioned goldfish bowls would be ideal for this job, especially as they are highly unsuitable for keeping goldfish.

Timber, in varying shapes and sizes is one of the most useful things we may salvage from the beach. It is the staple diet of a wrecker's day. From fish-boxes to ships' hatch-covers. I wonder how many old coastal cottages and houses did not have some beach timber built in somewhere. In the Isles of Scilly, every self-respecting farmer-fisherman has a wreck-pile from which he selects the required piece of wood for the job in hand (page 67).

Much of it is soft-wood, and very often irretrievably damaged by marine borers and fit only for the fire, but often enough you may find a nice piece of teak or oak on the beach. Perhaps a portion of deck cargo that has been washed away; when it is rain washed and dried

68

out there is a lifetime of use in it.

Not only cut timber, but the trees themselves may end up on the tide line. Torn by the roots in time of flood or avalanche, they are riverborne and finally seaborne. They may even carry large rocks in their roots so that eventually the rock alone is left, out of its geological context, to puzzle and intrigue. In studying Arctic sea currents it was found that stranded trees could be traced back to their home valleys. Different climates and different valleys produced a recognisable variation in the character of the tree rings so that a study of trees cut down *in situ* made it possible to identify the origin of tree trunks stranded a great distance away from home.

After heavy rains, great islands of floating reed mats may form in estuaries. They carry with them a rich assortment of vegetation and a floating oasis of unwilling animal voyagers. Tens of miles off the mouth of the river Congo, a young negro was once discovered sitting on a floating tree island of this sort. These mobile tropical islands are not infrequent and, sometimes massive enough to be a danger to shipping, are the subject of special 'Notices to Mariners'. One of the theories relating to the remote Pacific Galapagos Islands is that its unique flora and fauna was enriched over a long period by animals which arrived on vegetable islands formed in the Ecuadorian deltas, 600 miles away.

Nearer Britain, it is by no means unusual to see small mounds of debris floating downhill on our own estuaries, and it is reasonable to assume that they carry unwilling insect passengers. Often you see a pied or grey wagtail, or a herring gull, taking a ride and investigating the possibilities.

Tree roots often assume most intriguing shapes after they have been scoured by sea and sand. Mostly they have a serpentine appearance and many people have driftwood snakes on their mantlepieces. Others use a driftwood tree, scoured and sculptural, as a garden bird-table support.

Pit props are fairly common beach finds. Short cut sections of spruce, they often get washed overboard on passage as deck cargo from Scandinavian ports to South Wales. Early in February 1961, in a storm, for safety's sake a coaster deliberately cut adrift some 60,000

Herring Gull

Shelduck

Cormorant

Small waders

Oystercatcher

Heron

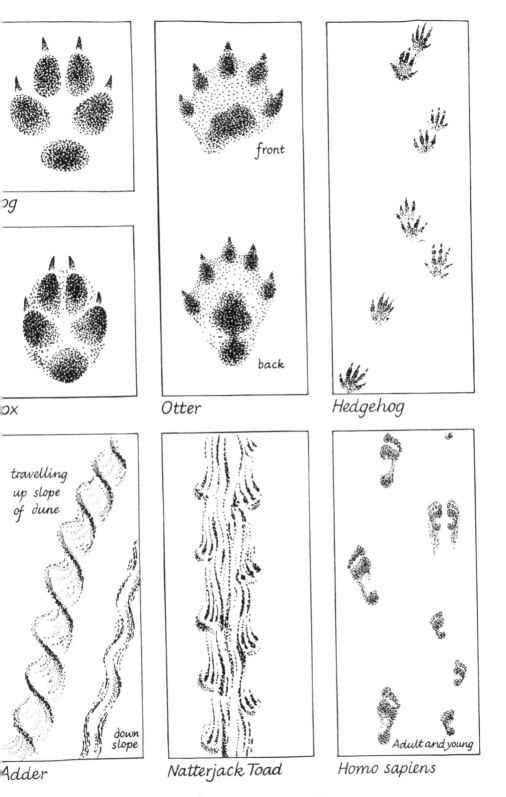

og

ox

Otter

front

back

Hedgehog

travelling
up slope
of dune

down
slope

Adder

Natterjack Toad

Adult and young

Homo sapiens

pit props which were travelling as deck cargo. They came ashore on the north Cornish coast which soon became a scene of intense activity. Many people were collecting the timber for firewood, but farmers, who have an infinite variety of uses for wreck, brought tractors and trailers in order to make greatest use of the windfall. One of the collectors was so enthusiastic he waded into the sea to reach the floating pit props. A big wave swept him off his feet and out to sea to a watery grave.

In dirty weather, an unprepared ship will lose a variety of gear from her deck. Hatch covers were, not so long ago, a fairly common and most useful discovery on the beach, but nowadays they are almost always made of slatted steel which has much greater strength and resistance to the grasping sea, so they remain firmly attached to the deck.

Again, after bad weather, it may happen that cargo from some long-sunk wreck may break out and litter a beach for miles. There is nothing quite so exciting as the sight of a stretch of beach spread with an assortment of broken and unbroken boxes and general chaos. Canned fruit, raisins, tobacco, wine casks, marine oil, tallow, the possibilities are endless, even if reality is not always quite so rewarding. A life-long wrecker once wrote to tell me of one such morning: '. . . just after the war there was some tobacco which came up in cases from a yankee liberty ship which broke up off here. I went early one morning with my nephew at first light, and stretched across the beach was case after case. We rushed down. I gave the first one a kick and heard tins rattling inside. I thought to myself, Corn in Egypt, which is a local saying if we thought we had struck it lucky. Took the lid off and they were filled with pint tins of Emergency Drinking Water, tinned in America, so that was a let down! We buried some in the dunes and used to tap them if we were thirsty.' This same man tells of many bales of rubber which may have come from a ship originally sunk in World War I. They weighed 100lb each, and although he got £5 each for them he reckoned he had earned it by the time he got them off the beach and up the cliff. He believes that quite a lot of people make a good living from wrecking.

However, there is a whole world of interest in a piece of timber which is not worth a penny piece. Examine the tatty and long-travelled pieces of wood on the shore and you will very often find that they have been carrying passengers which were not at all pleased to reach land. (Incidentally, there is an ocean going fish which is commonly found sheltering underneath drifting timber, and it bears the highly suitable name of wreck fish.) During its time at sea the surface of floating wood may have been colonised by creatures which, floating about in the plankton, were looking for a more permanent home. Acorn barnacles and goose barnacles are most likely to be found on the outside surfaces. The goose barnacles, curious beasts with a striking likeness to the head and neck of a bird, are stalked barnacles which have cemented themselves to the timber during its time in warmer parts of the Atlantic. In the days of slow-moving ships they attached themselves in numbers underneath the waterline and then grew fat, doing no good to the vessel's hydrodynamic shape and much reducing her speed.

Ocean currents finally land these timber-borne crustaceans on our temperate shores, and weakened by the increasing chill they soon die when they are exposed to the air. Sometimes the individuals in the cluster are little finger nail size, sometimes several inches long and in such profusion that you can hardly see the wood to which they are attached. The curious shape and featheriness of goose barnacles is responsible for the widely held belief, in medieval times, that after growing on trees they subsequently hatched into geese. Certainly the barnacle goose has a somewhat similar shape and colour and is a coastal bird, but that is about as far as the relationship goes. From the medieval layman's point of view the belief had the advantage of allowing barnacle geese to be eaten on Fridays; hatched from a sea creature, they were classified as fish.

Barnacles congregate on the outside of drifting timber, but there are other creatures which are active inside. They are of special interest to mariners because they can cause a great deal of damage and, indeed, in severe cases they may cause a ship to founder. Since the earliest days of civilisation ships have suffered from the attacks of 'worm'. Fouling by barnacles and seaweed reduced the speed of a ship and was dealt with by regular careening and scraping, but until the sheathing of underwater hulls with copper no one could counter the destructive marine borers. It was found that the interaction of sea water with the copper produced a slow release of copper salt solution which was toxic to the ship-worm. Copper is expensive, so today the work of discouraging attack by marine borers is done by anti-fouling paints which still use the same principle of slowly releasing a toxic copper salt solution.

The pieces of wood thrown up on the beach are unlikely to have been protected by anti-fouling paint, and are very often extensively damaged by the most common of the borers, ship worm and gribble (see page 75). The gribble, despite his rather attractive name, is a voracious beast, a crustacean isopod looking much like a miniature beach sandhopper. It attacks wood from the surface, making minute holes of about $\frac{1}{8}$in diameter and then excavating shallow galleries about $\frac{1}{10}$in deep. Because it is so numerous the galleries soon merge together, the surface of the timber is destroyed, and the timber gets wetter and softer. Jetty and pier piling subjected to this kind of attack may eventually collapse altogether.

The ship worm—teredo—is not a worm at all, but a particularly destructive bivalve mollusc. It certainly looks like a worm, and may be as much as 1 ft long, but at the end of its body is its shell, greatly reduced in size; a highly specialised boring device. It penetrates timber in its larval stage, making a very small entrance hole. Once inside it takes a smart right-angle turn and then digs out a tunnel lengthways just inside the surface, so that although you cannot see it, it is literally eating the plank, or whatever, away. The teredo cuts the tunnel as it grows, burrowing with a twisting movement of the shell. There are three species in British waters, the largest, *Teredo norvegicus*, is also the commonest. It is rather more common in the south than in the north, and is most active from April through to October. In the tropics there are species which grow up to 5ft long, a horrid thought for any boat owner.

The gribble effect is easy to spot, but teredo may only be revealed by splitting the timber open, although the presence of many small round cleanly cut holes is a clue. The result of splitting a well eaten log is quite spectacular. If the wood is newly cast ashore it is more

74

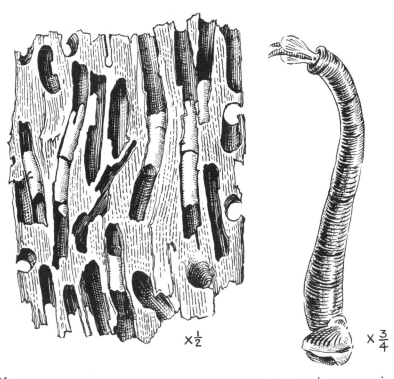

x ½

x ¾

SHIPWORM *Teredo norvegica*
Timber-boring bivalve

x 2

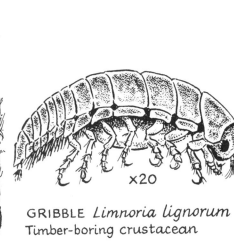

x20

GRIBBLE *Limnoria lignorum*
Timber-boring crustacean

likely that you will see the complete worm, but if it has been out of the sea some time you will have to look carefully to see the remains of the beast—just the cutting edges, the two shells. Teredo attacks wooden pier piling too, and it is an animal to be taken very seriously.

Small boats, at least, are rapidly becoming made of glass reinforced plastics, and this is one way of reducing the likelihood of damage by gribble and teredo. Teredo has been known to attack plastics, so it may be that in the long run it even learns to deal with the new breed of yachtsmen, but there is no doubt that beaches are going to be less rewarding places for wreckers as the GRP revolution continues. An old wooden ship gently rotting on a beach provides a quantity of interest, both in natural phenomena and from the pleasure of seeing the harmonious construction of the keel, frames and planking. But we must adapt to the change and learn to enjoy the plastic artefacts which decorate the tide line, detergent bottles and flip-flop shoes which may have come from far off places and stretch our command of lan-

Plastic seaweed in the test tank. The mound of sand on the right has been deposited downstream of the seaweed, which encourages sand accumulation.

guage to read their inscriptions. Sometimes they too will have bristle worms and barnacles attached to them, and jammed in the right place they may provide a home for a crab or an anemone.

But perhaps the strangest innovation is plastic seaweed, which I suppose in due course may also become a common strandline object after storms, like its natural progenitor. The original idea is said to have come from a Danish fisherman, who noticed the way seaweed has a calming effect on the sea. Developed in order to combat coastal erosion, loss of sand in particular, the weed is made of 8ft lengths of polypropylene tape, looking something like thongweed (page 76). Tufts of the tape are attached at one yard intervals to lengths of steel chain, and then laid in rows at right-angles to the shore. The experiment has been tried in the USA and in Holland and Britain (in Yorkshire, Suffolk and Hampshire). Preliminary tests in the sheltered Danish waters resulted in a 1 metre build-up of sand over a period of 18 months. Apart from the obvious value to seaside holiday resorts, it may be that plastic seaweed will prevent erosion and undermining around deep-water pipelines, possibly protect experimental fish breeding grounds and help with the delicate operation of encouraging oyster spat to anchor themselves. However the most difficult problem is apparently to anchor the 'seaweed' itself successfully.

It is difficult to imagine anything more exotic than plastic seaweed on a beach, yet tropical beans are strong contenders. There are two species which arrive on western coasts not infrequently, and they come here after a long Atlantic journey which starts in the Caribbean. A glance at the surface current chart (page 23) shows the route. Both of them are hard and tough objects, but I imagine they would need both those qualities to make such a long passage without being eaten or otherwise attacked. Both are about the size of a large broad bean; one of them, *Entada gigas*, is the same shape. It is a seed which comes from the West Indies, has a uniform brown colour and a hard shiny skin. The other, *Mucuna urens*, shaped more like a disc, has a black creamy bordered rim on a dark purple-brown background. It probably comes from Central America. John Barrett, the marine biologist, says that in his home county of Pembrokeshire parents give the Caribbean bean to babies for them to cut their teeth on. And we always keep one in the wheelhouse of our boat, in respect to the belief that it will save us from drowning! If you want to do the same it will take some perseverance, because tropical beans are not easily found. If you cannot wait to find one, then David Hunt, who organises wildlife holidays in the Isles of Scilly and is a keen bean man, will sell you one at a modest price. It will certainly serve for your baby's teeth, but I do not know if a bought bean will save you from a watery grave, and I trust you never put it to the test.

Sometimes deep sea jellyfish are stranded on our beaches in large numbers. This happens, mainly on western coasts, after a long period in which south-west winds have persistently blown them towards us. Both the species stranded this way are by-the-wind sailing creatures, unable to govern their own movements in the way used by the common jellyfish, which swims by opening and closing its discs, thereby producing a sort of slow motion jet propulsion.

The first is called the 'by-the-wind-sailor' and is somewhat like our own well-known jellyfish but more oval and with a hard ridge 'sail' which extends right across a diameter. Deep blue round the edge, it is 4in or so across. The second is the Portuguese man-o'-war, which is a most wonderfully constructed creature. The bladder, which is the part you are most likely to find on the beach (page 79) is up to about 6in long, and looks very much like some kind of child's balloon. Indeed it can be difficult to persuade someone that it is animal and not man made. The float is a pale blue, and there is a crenellated crest of a pinkish colour. From the float hangs a complicated cluster of stinging cells in long tentacles. If the jellyfish is alive, do not touch it as it can deliver a powerful sting. This is its method of capturing its prey—small fish—in the ocean. Very often the animal is somewhat battered by the time it reaches our shores, and the bladder is the only part left. When they do appear, it may well be in very large numbers over a long stretch of coastline.

Home grown jellyfish are frequently stranded. *Aurelia* is the commonest, usually about 6–8in across, with its four purple rings. A larger, and stinging, animal is *Chrysaora*, milky-white with a central brown spot and radial brown streaks. Then there is *Rhizostoma*, the biggest, up to 2ft across and quite harmless; it is pale green or blue,

Stranded Portuguese man-o'-war

with a darker purple fringe.

A regularly found object on the beach is the 'bone' of one of the cuttlefish species. A carnivorous beast, the cuttlefish is a complex mollusc related to squid and octopus. Unlike the more familiar snails, which carry their shells on their backs, cuttlefish are actually built around their shells. And it is these shells which end up on the strand-line. The living creature has five pairs of tentacles with suckers which it uses for seizing prey. Leslie Jackman, who runs the aquarium by Paignton Harbour, once had a cuttlefish which would take prawns from his hand, rather like a robin coming for a mealworm. It would approach slowly, changing colour as it moved and betrayed its emotion, jet propelling itself by forcing water through a funnel formed by its foot, then suddenly seize the prey and deliver it to the

79

parroty beak of its mouth. Striped almost in zebra fashion, the common cuttlefish may be up to 12in long. The other species are smaller, round about the 2–5in mark. They are widely distributed and common, especially on southern coasts. The scientific name *Sepia* describes the dark brown fluid taken from a small ink sac inside the animal. It was used for ink by the Greeks and Romans.

Cuttle bone is well known to all budgerigar fanciers. In fact it is in short supply at the moment; a year or so ago it cost the wholesaler 25 pence a pound, but now it has doubled if they can get it at all. Most comes from Portugal, where the flesh of the cuttlefish was bought by housewives and the bone exported to Britain, after being dried on special racks in the sun or treated to infra-red heat. Some was imported from France, and at one time annual imports were of the order of 100 tons—a figure almost as surprising as the belief that budgerigars are now the most-kept pet in England.

If you think of giving a beach-found cuttle bone to your budgie, bear in mind that, according to the experts, no superior fancier would dream of it. The dirt and grit embedded in the beach specimen might encourage disease. All the same, beach cuttle bones very often, to the naked eye at least, seem the very essence of purity, and it seems you may give it to your cage-bird after you have washed it thoroughly and heated it in a slow oven to kill the bugs. If you have a lot of cuttle bones on your beach and think you might make a fortune by selling to one of the big cage-bird suppliers then I wish you luck, and tell you that the smallest quantity that will interest them is several hundredweights.

There are other sea-washed and sun-dried shells to be found on the beach, and how curious that there is nothing macabre about them; they are so perfect and clean that instead of the sort of reaction one half expects in touching mortal remains there is a pleasure in the delicate colouring and structure. Even the empty shell of a spiny spider crab, a harmless beast which gives plenty of people the creepie-crawlies while it is alive, is a pleasure to examine. If it is freshly ashore then it may still have anemones, sea squirts, sponges and barnacles growing in among the prickles of its back. Then there is the red case of the edible crab and the green one of the shore crab. If they are still in the stage of internal decomposition then they will be providing food for strandline scavengers like turnstones and sand-hoppers.

After a storm you may find the washed up tests of the sea potato, a sea urchin which in the live state lives in a sandy burrow offshore in deep water. Not very much like the common sea urchin, whose hard red test is sold in souvenir shops in the form of lamp bases, this one is near-white and very fragile. It has a resemblance to a skull, and the thin hollow shell is marked with five rows of small holes. Sea mice, too, may suddenly appear on the shore line in vast numbers. A slug-shaped worm 3–4in long, it has iridescent green and golden hairs and bristly toothbrush legs.

Mermaid's purses are one of the more romantic things to find (page 82). They are the used egg cases of dogfish, rays and skate. Deposited by the female and lashed by the tendrils to the fronds or stalks of kelp at extreme low-water mark, they grow and finally hatch, leaving the purse to be broken free and cast ashore. Sometimes there will be a disaster and the egg breaks free too soon, and the unfortunate remains of the embryo will still be inside the leathery egg case when you find it.

The spongy yellow egg masses of the common whelk (page 82) are common on beaches. Varying in size from a golf ball to a football, they too are usually empty and the juvenile whelks have gone before the egg capsules reach the beach, having been torn from their rock anchorages by turbulence. But there may be a certain amount of yolk left, so open them gently (because you may find they squirt liquid at you; sailors and longshoremen have been known to use them instead of soap) and there may well be castaways like long-clawed porcelain crabs hiding inside. These are about the size of your little finger nail, but they have broad prizefighter's arms. Normally they are found in kelp holdfasts, but it seems that whelk egg masses have an attraction for them. I once examined fifty of the masses on a beach and found that all but six had the little crabs nestling inside, many of them still alive.

Over a period of time a great quantity of dead and decomposing animal and vegetable matter gets thrown ashore on beaches, but the

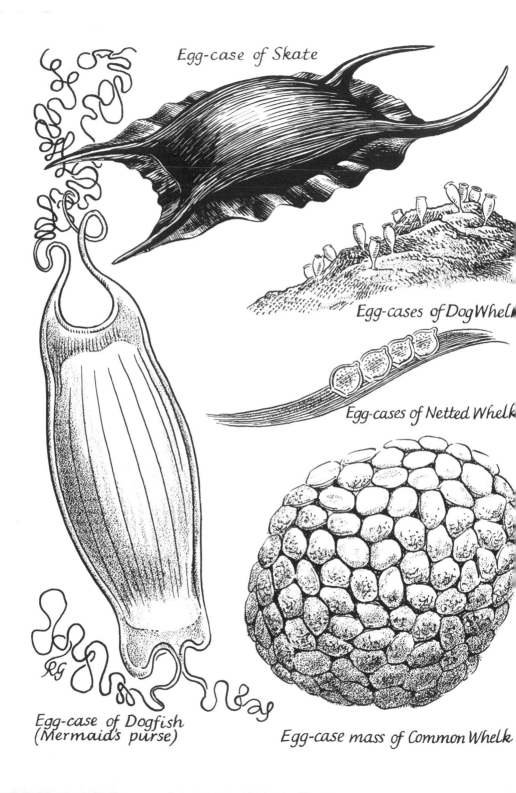

Egg-case of Skate

Egg-cases of DogWhelk

Egg-cases of Netted Whelk

Egg-case of Dogfish
(Mermaid's purse)

Egg-case mass of Common Whelk

scavengers are well able to deal with it. Gulls and turnstones do their bit, but the master cleaners are the great armies of sandhoppers which live in the sand and decaying seaweed during the day, and leap about in the search for food at night. Their many legs are made for jumping as well as walking (they are called beach fleas in America) and they are to be seen in clouds sometimes, as they make their way down to the fertile lower parts of the beach at low water. They are powerful feeders. I left a pair of woollen bathing pants on the beach by mistake one night. Next morning they were a ragged mass of holes.

Pieces of string full of holes are most likely to be torn pieces of fishing net. Nowadays they are likely to be made from synthetic twines, and highly coloured in orange or blue. They will be from trawl or seine or trammel nets, or possibly even from crab pots, and will be of varying sizes. There are strict laws governing the mesh used to catch fish. For instance in Britain there is an absolute ban on mesh sizes between 50 and 70 millimetres. Below 50mm the nets are for pelagic—open water—fish and for shrimps and sprats; above 70mm for demersal—bottom feeding—fish. But you are likely to find almost any size on the beach. Unfortunately, the better quality synthetic lines such as nylon and terylene, which would be a welcome find, have a high specific gravity and sink to be lost for ever, whereas the cheaper and less useful polythene and polypropylene versions float for ever, sometimes to wrap themselves around boat propellers with dire results. Nylon fishing line of the type used by anglers comes ashore in dangerous little balls, usually wrapped in a bundle of seaweed which it has torn adrift, providing buoyancy.

Plaited polythene is used a great deal by deep-sea trawlers, and to some extent in small trawls and gill nets. Synthetic line comes in a bewildering number of forms, and with an equally bewildering number of functions, but we can say that polypropylene twines tend to be of a natural colour, or green or brown, and that polythene comes plaited or twisted and orange in colour. These are the ones most likely to be found on the beach. Black polythene is used for crab pot netting because it is less susceptible to damage by the ultra-violet rays of direct sunlight when the pots are out of the water. It is the main disadvantage of synthetic lines that, if left in hot sun, they may deteriorate to a condition where they will collapse without warning. But, on the other side of the coin, they are strong, weather-resistant and less liable to swell up in the wet than natural fibre ropes.

The iron, glass and plastic floats used by fishermen are one of the commonest beach finds (page 85). I used to have a collie bitch whose greatest delight was to see one while it was still drifting; she would swim out and turn it over and over until she got a grip on the eye lug, and then bring it ashore to play football and bark. Often when you find them on the shore the lug is broken but this is less likely with the incredibly tough new plastic versions.

The various kinds of floats are used to hold fishing nets upright in the water and they are counter-balanced by lead or chain sinkers which pull the nets downward to the sea bed. Many floats come from trawls —enormous bags of netting with a great mouth perhaps 80ft across. The lower lip, a weighted foot-rope, sweeps the bottom, the mouth held open by otter boards which sheer out like submarine kites as the apparatus is towed along. The upper lip, or head-rope, is kept up with a row of floats. These may have to withstand enormous pressure, and that is one reason for their invariable ball shape. Seiners and some trawlers fish in depths of up to 60 fathoms; their floats are anything from 5–10in in diameter with a single welded lug. In Arctic waters trawlers may be working as deep as 300 fathoms, so it is clear that the trawl floats, although much the same size as the shallow water versions, have to be strong. These floats always used to be made of galvanised iron or aluminium, and since there are large numbers in circulation this kind is likely to be coming ashore for a long while yet. Some of them have one or more metal rims around the outside. These are specially designed to impart an upwards planing movement when the trawl is being towed forwards. Some steel floats are painted but the aluminium ones are always the natural grey colour, and have the advantage that they do not corrode. All British metal floats are made in Grimsby. Buoyancies range from about 2lb for a 5in diameter steel float to about 14lb for a 10in aluminium alloy one.

For some years now there has been a swing towards a plastic float, which superficially looks the same. There was some doubt about their suitability when they first appeared, and salesmen had to be con-

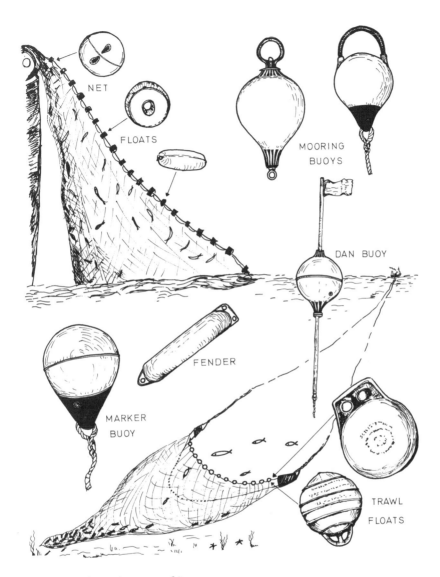

NET

FLOATS

MOORING
BUOYS

DAN BUOY

FENDER

MARKER
BUOY

TRAWL
FLOATS

Buoys and floats (not to scale)

85

vinced of their value. At the headquarters of the famous Bridport Gundry works in Dorset, a group of representatives was taken to the Board Room and shown the new toys. These were a hollow plastic float made in one piece of a very hard, impact-resisting plastic, coloured white or light orange, with buoyancies of up to 9lb and a maximum working depth of 500 fathoms. The salesmen were not too impressed, and were invited to throw them out of the first floor window to an asphalt drive below. After an afternoon's efforts, during which very little other work got done, they only managed to break one float. The galvanised version was doomed. Bridport Gundry claim that their 'permolift supa' trawl floats have a distinctive orange colour which is ideal for night fishing under arc lamps, and that in daylight the colour appears neutral to fish.

The floats originate from almost any European country, mainly from Norway, but some come from as far as the Far East, and the embossed designs can be very attractive. Usually they include the maker's name and country of origin, and sometimes they bear a figure indicating tested working depth, for instance 'prof. 800m'.

Seine nets may be floated by dozens of cork 'doughnuts' or by as many as thirty of the well-known glass floats—fortune teller's globes of green, brown, or blue translucence. Nowadays these too are being superseded by ball or egg-shaped plastic floats, and the corks by similarly shaped PVC or polystyrene. Some fishermen like to use the cork floats still because, after a lifetime of experience, they know exactly how many to use to get the kind of buoyancy they need. But there is not much doubt that there will be fewer and fewer corks and glass balls in use and inevitably fewer coming ashore. The expanded PVC or polystyrene floats, whether of solid or hollow construction, are almost ideal for the job, being impervious to water and highly resistant to weathering. They are made in a wide variety of colours, which certainly adds something to the wrecking scene.

Floats of solid construction are mainly from Norway, while Denmark was the first country to introduce the hollow plastic version; grey-coloured spheres from 3–8in in diameter, with grooved holes instead of lugs for attaching to the head-line.

This grooved type is now also made in Britain, white or grey for deep-water trawls and orange for use on seine nets in depths up to about 100 fathoms. Then again there is a very commonly used Norwegian soft PVC material buoy, orange-coloured and ball-shaped, with a single moulded lug. This is designed for use in shallow water. For the same purpose there are expanded polystyrene solid floats of a mottled blue-grey colour, made in Norway for use on surface float-lines. These solid floats come in a bewildering variety of sizes and shapes—egg, ball, cylinder—and with a variety of holes and grooves. Mostly they are small by comparison with the trawl floats.

Like the galvanised trawl floats, the glass balls will inevitably be less common on beaches, and will perhaps become collectors' pieces. One of the pleasures of early morning wrecking used to be the colourful glistenings of a glass float in the wet sand and the low sun. It is true that you can buy a bowdlerised version in souvenir shops, but these are of inferior and fragile construction, and the string netting which encloses them is a poor thing compared with the kind made of codline by a fisherman. Not surprisingly perhaps, the souvenir shop float costs rather more than the commercial variety! When I collected wrecked floats ten years ago in the Isles of Scilly the going retail rate was a shilling each for a genuine one. We used to think it a monstrous price, and were sorry for the tourists. Now the souvenir shops sell their version for 34 pence, a 700 per cent increase for an inferior product.

Cork still comes ashore in fair quantity, helped along by its buoyant attitude to the sea. In times past, to prevent the cramp, people used a cork garter round the leg or slept with a piece under the mattress. If you want to try this, then a determined search of the tide line should find you a piece. Sometimes you will find a piece of cork bark from which a row of suspiciously wine-bottle cork shaped holes has been cut. How they get into the sea I don't know, and should welcome information.

Dan buoys, sometimes known as dhan, or danh, are the marker buoys, often with a flag on top, which mark the end position of set nets or longlines. They may be Heath Robinson affairs made of a few cork doughnuts threaded and lashed to a stick, or they may be of cylindrical polystyrene, about a foot in diameter and 15in high; or spherical or pear shaped. The most expensive ones are made of inflated PVC. They are very tough and weather resistant and are brightly coloured to make them easy to locate from a distance. They may be anything from 40 to over 100 inches in circumference. The same inflated PVC technique is used for a number of other types of marker and mooring buoys and some of them used as fenders. In fact, you need to bear in mind that, while manufacturers may well make floats for a specific purpose, they will undoubtedly be used in practice for any number of different jobs. A distant-waters trawl float constructed to withstand sea pressure at 400 fathoms may end life after many vicissitudes as a surface marker, connected by a piece of strandline polythene to a crab pot in 5 fathoms of water. Fishermen are master wreckers!

Modern dan buoys should bear a sequence of letters and numbers which represent the fishing boat's registration mark. Returned to the Receiver of Wreck they attract a reward. Because of the greatly increased activity of coastal shipping, new legislation will enforce fishing vessels to mark their gear more conscientiously. Better and more conspicuous marking of longlines, trammels and crab pots would certainly be popular with anyone who has to make coastal passages in boats. At the moment it is like trying to thread an inshore maze, there are so many poorly marked and dangerous floating lines on the sea.

Cork or plastic lifebuoys and liferafts are exciting discoveries. If the name of the ship and port of registry is legible then you should report them immediately to the nearest coastguard in case they represent news of value. Mostly they have been lost overboard in undramatic circumstances but you can never be sure until you have checked.

One of the less attractive habits of ship masters, naval and commercial alike, is that of jettisoning 'gash' at sea. Sooner or later a lot of it finds its way ashore to litter the beaches. On her way home to Portsmouth for paying-off, one well-known naval vessel dumped a quantity of unwanted material overboard. The north-west gale which was blowing at the time carried masses of papers to the island of Alderney, where the fields were soon spread with them. The States of

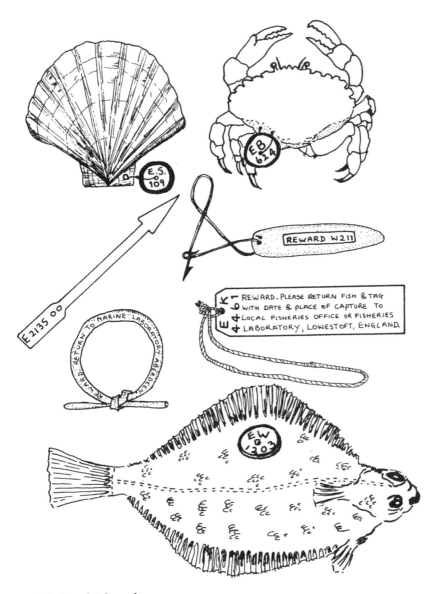

Labels visible within the illustration:

E.S.
109

EB
624

REWARD W211

E 2135 00

E K 4 6 1 — REWARD. PLEASE RETURN FISH & TAG WITH DATE & PLACE OF CAPTURE TO LOCAL FISHERIES OFFICE OR FISHERIES LABORATORY, LOWESTOFT, ENGLAND.

REWARD. RETURN TO MARINE LABORATORY, ABERDEEN

EW 1303

Shellfish and fish marks

Alderney had to get the Public Works Department to round them up for incineration, but confirmed wreckers now have their own complete copies of useless but intriguing Standing Orders.

Sailors seem to make a habit of throwing electric light bulbs away, and in spite of their delicate nature they often end up on the strand-line intact. As an exercise, I brought three of them home the other day and tried them in a mains socket. Incredibly, two of them worked, albeit with some ominous fizzing.

A certain amount of food is thrown overboard or lost overboard from ships, and not all of it is recycled by the gulls before it reaches the shore. An extraordinary coincidence in this connection was told me by Mrs Barbara Benton of the Channel Island of Alderney. Early in 1972 two half-pint cartons of milk, still full, sailed in and landed on an Alderney beach. They were labelled 'Alderney Puritan Milk' yet were packed in Chicago. The curious part of the story is that since the last war there have been, alas, no Alderney cows (a breed in the same sense that Jersey and Guernsey cattle are separate) on the island, and that they only exist in America, where shipments were sent in 1890 and 1910. A strange coincidence that Alderney milk should find its way back home, presumably lost overboard from a ship in the channel. Milk is an unlikely sort of thing to find on a beach, but on hot days I have eaten, with relish, grapefruit and oranges from the strandline. I draw the line at the extraordinary number of onions we sometimes see, and wait with eternal hope for the traditional barrel of rum.

Fish sometimes turn up on the beach dead, though I think it would be a brave man who ate them, because the flesh deteriorates very fast indeed. It is well worth looking to see whether they carry a metal or plastic number tag—evidence that they are part of a scientific investigation. In Britain the operational headquarters is the Fisheries Laboratory in Lowestoft. The work is planned and co-ordinated by the Ministry of Agriculture Fisheries and Food, using research vessels and sometimes chartered commercial vessels. Fish marking experiments are being carried out in all the major fisheries extending from Spitsbergen to the Irish Sea and Western Approaches. In addition to herring, five of the commoner bottom fish are marked on a large scale—cod, haddock, whiting, plaice and sole. The object of the exercise is to discover the effect of fishing on fish populations, that is to discover what proportion of a fish stock is being caught. Long term management, whether by mesh regulation or by closure of certain grounds or other controls, depends on knowledge of this kind.

Naturally, the great proportion of fish tag recoveries is by fishermen themselves, but not infrequently the tags end up ashore. A Russian tag, No 27082, was placed on a cod which was released off Labrador in 1963; it was eventually recovered by a small boy on Torcross beach in Devon, in 1969. In more local fish-marking experiments tags often come to be found by beachcombers.

There are various types of mark (page 89); disc, hook or tag, and various materials used; metal, celluloid or plastic. Experiments have shown that different species of fish each have a tag and tag position which suits them best. In the case of plastic flags, the material is impregnated with an anti-fouling compound to inhibit marine organisms from attachment. The treatment is necessary because in British waters the tags were sometimes recovered with 15cm of weed attached, a somewhat unfair load for the fish to drag around.

Crabs and scallops have also been the subject of marking experiments, although in the case of crabs a difficulty arises when the tag is cast off with the periodic moult. Shellfish or fish tags, if possible complete with owner, should be delivered to the nearest Fishery Office or to the Fisheries Laboratory, Lowestoft, giving date and position of recovery, and any other relevant information.

Bird rings may be found on the shore, so if ever you see a dead bird check its legs. And, sadly, dead birds are only too common around our coasts nowadays. The auk family, the guillemots and razorbills, are the most likely if there has been an oil spillage, but at one time or another you will see most of the seabirds on the British List, dead from a variety of causes—rough weather, food shortages, chemicals and unknown factors. Auks are the most seriously affected by oil because they have the unfortunate habit of spending a lot of their migration time on the surface of the sea when they are on passage to and from the breeding cliffs and the wintering quarters around the Iberian Peninsula and the open Atlantic. They are gregarious birds,

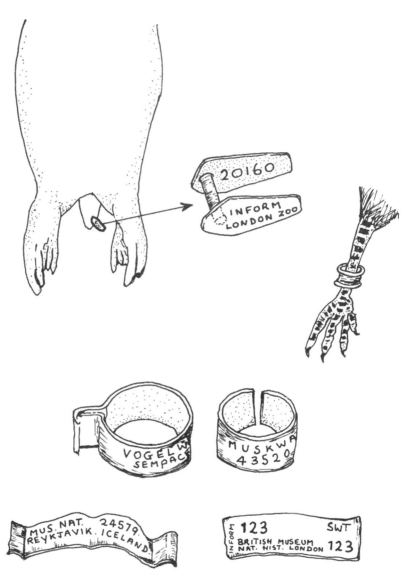

Seal and bird tags and rings. Seal tags, with information on place, date, species, should be returned to the Seal Research Unit, Fisheries Laboratory, Lowestoft. Bird rings, with information, to the British Trust for Ornithology, Beech Grove, Tring, Herts.

they paddle about and socialise, and if they are unlucky they swim into oil patches. The oil gets their feathers in a mess; they preen; and once oil is in their lungs they are very likely doomed. Eventually the sad black-and-white corpse comes ashore. Only a small proportion of ringed birds is recovered, so every recovery is of real value. Send the ring, flattened and stuck to your letter containing information about species, place and date, to the British Trust for Ornithology, Beech Grove, Tring, Hertfordshire.

Both grey and common seals have been ringed or tagged for some years now and, as for dead birds, it is always important to check a seal body in case it is tagged. In the early days we used a monel metal ring, somewhat similar to a bird ring, and clipped it over the 'thumb' of either of the hind flippers. But now there is a much more efficient method which uses cattle tags attached to the seal's tail.

If you do find a dead seal, whether ringed or not, you should report the discovery, including details of place, date, species, sex and age of the animal (if you can manage it!) to the Seals Research Unit, c/o Fisheries Laboratory, Lowestoft, Suffolk.

Your chance of finding a tagged turtle is somewhat on the slim side, but turtles are marked and they do occasionally get stranded on European coasts; in one bumper year there were eleven recorded in Britain alone! A metal tag may be attached to the hind border of one of the front flippers, but up till now only adult turtles have been marked (by scientists in the USA and Mexico) and these are less likely to reach our shores. If ever one is found, however, it will be valuable proof of its origin. It is well known that loggerhead turtles make regular journeys into the Atlantic, and it seems likely that young turtles have on occasion been swept off course by Caribbean hurricanes, then carried to Europe by the North Atlantic Current. If this is the case, then the journey may take well over a year.

Lastly we come to the possibility of finding a stranded whale. Continuous records have been kept since 1913, and an average year may see something like fifty whales coming ashore. Many of them are still alive. It is not easy to determine why these great beasts find themselves in such a parlous state. Perhaps nothing more complicated than that they find themselves stranded by a falling tide on a shelving

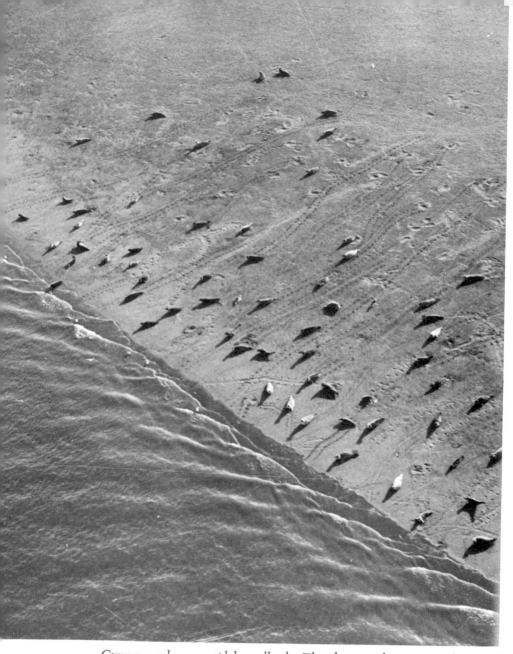

Common seals on a tidal sandbank. They leave a characteristic drag mark flanked by regular flipper marks on either side.

beach. Although they are air breathing mammals and can survive for quite long periods out of the water, the danger is that they may get overheated or that because of sheer unsupported weight out of water their lungs collapse. Because this is less of a problem to them, the smaller species, like dolphins, survive much longer out of water. Attempts have been made, all unsuccessfully as far as I know, to tow stranded cetaceans out to sea again in an effort to save them.

Where large numbers are stranded, the species is more often than not the pilot whale, but individual members of many other species have been recorded at one time or another. Some of the records are astonishing, like the two narwhals which beached by the Thames in 1949. Arctic animals, these were the first British records for 128 years.

Whales are technically Royal Fish and, as such, stranded specimens are dealt with by the Receiver of Wreck under the Wreck Regulations. Sturgeon are included in the Receiver's responsibility, but other large fish, carcasses, etc. are the province of the Public Health Officer. (In Scotland whales of the species known as bottlenose and caa'ing and also those of a length less than 25ft from tip to tail, are not Royal Fish and are not claimed on behalf of the Crown.)

Pilot whale stranded on the north Cornish coast. Pet owners started to cut free dog meat from the carcase until the Receiver stepped in. Important data are collected by Natural History Museum scientists from strandings of this sort.

Fishes Royal are so called because by ancient usage they were the prerogative of the king—a tithe rendered to him in return for guarding the seas and protecting the coasts from pirates and robbers. They belong to the Crown not only when stranded but also when caught in territorial waters. Although the practice dates back to Plantagenet times the first recorded example in the English language is of an Elizabethan lawyer who writes in 1570 of 'great or roialle fishe, as whales or such other, which by the Lawe of Prerogative pertain to the King himselfe'. Edward I declared that the whole sturgeon was reserved for the king, but that in the case of a whale the king should have the head, the queen the tail and the captors the carcass. But Edward II made a clean sweep and proclaimed: 'The King shall have wreck of the sea throughout the Realm'.

We may wonder what value the king received from the unfortunate whales cast ashore, but it is as well for all of us that the Crown recognises responsibility for disposal of the remains. The Royal Navy has often done the job with explosives, but it can be a difficult task, especially in remote places. Mostly they are towed out to sea and sunk.

Detailed records have been kept of stranded whales, dolphins and porpoises for many years. Because cetaceans are difficult to study 'in the field' there has always been a keen scientific interest in the carcasses. Coastguards and Receivers of Wreck report to the British Museum (Natural History) in London, using a specially compiled report form which details a great deal of information about the species, size, shape, colour and other useful data. Sometimes they send portions of the carcass or even the whole specimen, although in the case of the larger whales this is somewhat less likely!

If you are the first to discover a stranded whale, inform the nearest coastguard. He will know what to do. Do not start to extract whale meat for your pet's dinner, for you will have the Keeper of Zoology hot foot from South Kensington, not to mention the Receiver of Wreck from the nearest Custom House.

4 The gourmet beachcomber

Grapefruit and oranges are often washed ashore, and a case of corned beef or TV dinners is entirely possible, but if you are going to rely on shipwrecked food, your life as a desert island castaway will be short. Fortunately, the seashore offers more easily available wild food than any other habitat. Cut off from the family fortunes without a penny, and reluctant to work, you could sustain yourself indefinitely on beach food. Meat and vegetables are there for the collecting, and provided you operate as a natural part of the community, farming the crop in such a way that it is maintained, you should continue for your allotted span.

Few of us are likely to become quite such dedicated longshore vagabonds, but there is a great deal of enjoyment and pleasure in collecting food from the beach. Much of it also happens to taste very good. Raw seaweed is perfectly edible, while somewhat tough and salty, but on the other hand a dish of scallops or clams, with sea beet, is fit for a king.

Coastal plants have often been the forerunners of more important cultivated varieties. For instance the cabbage tribe is derived from sea kale. Mangold wurzels, sugar beet and beet-root are cultivated versions of the sea beet.

Sea beet is a common, though somewhat scattered and solitary, coarse perennial. The 2–3ft long stems lie along the ground at the lowest plant zone on spray washed cliffs, or just above the highest strandline, particularly on shingle. It enjoys disturbed ground, for instance at the edges of a car park or caravan site, or on cliff falls. It is especially large and luxurious where it gets the benefit of seabird droppings on the grand scale, for instance at the foot of a breeding bird cliff. Seabird droppings are wonderfully rich in phosphates and nitrogen, although on occasion they can be somewhat too much of a good thing when they smother the vegetation. The young leaves of sea beet are protein rich, and have a high vitamin A content, but what is more they are delicious. You need to collect rather a lot (like spinach). Wash thoroughly, cut off any thick stems, and boil in a little salted water (cover the bottom of the pan only) for about 20 minutes. The leaves are full of moisture, and if you put the lid on the saucepan there will be plenty of water to do the cooking. Drain and press. Chop with butter and a little black pepper. It has a rich taste, not so acid as spinach, which is of course the cultivated form. Sea beet does well in garden soil, incidentally.

Both orache and sea kale can be eaten like spinach. Orache is a purely coastal plant, typical of the drift zone on sand and shingle foreshore. Sea kale was at one time extensively cultivated in Britain. Now relatively rare, it is found on sand or shingle beaches, most frequently at the eastern end of the south coast. The young shoots are eaten like asparagus after the plant has been blanched—keeping the light away by building a pile of shingle over it.

Fennel grows on sea cliffs; the leaves can be used for fish sauces and soups and salad dressings. Oil extracted from the aromatic fruits has various uses for condiment manufacturers and confectioners, and the fruits are listed in the British Pharmaceutical Codex as a cure for flatulence! The most famous of the edible plants is rock samphire, a tender green stalk a couple of feet high, branching out into numbers of thick round leaves. The white flowers, in July and August, are followed by seeds something like those of fennel. The root is very large and white. The plant grows on and above the spray zone on rocky cliffs, and also on sand and shingle. Both leaves and root have a hot spicy taste, and at one time they were much used for making pickle. 'Crest marine' was the cry in London streets. William Borlase, writing of the natural history of Cornwall in the eighteenth century, said 'Among the rock and cliff-plants the Samphire may be reckoned the most useful. Some boil it as a pot-herb; pickled, it is thought to help digestion: Dr Leigh thinks it may be ranked in the first class of antiscorbutics.' It also has a rich iodine content. In Culpeper's *Herbal*, he adjures us all to take it as a remedy for the 'ill digestions and obstructions [which] are the cause of most of the diseases which the frail nature of man is subject to'. Shakespeare has the hard-pressed King Lear look over the cliff to where 'half-way down hangs one that gathers samphire, dreadful trade'.

There is another samphire, no less enjoyable, which grows more commonly in estuaries. The succulent, salt-tolerant marsh samphire, or glasswort, is a pioneer plant, colonising mud at about high-water mark where there is not much current. It is small, just a few inches high, but a thick juicy little plant, bright translucent green slightly tinged with red and yellow. Like seaweed, in the past it was burnt and the ash provided soda for the process of glass making. Pick the most succulent, usually the shortest, pieces. Wash, boil in salted water for ten minutes or so. Dip the sprigs into melted butter, then suck them off the stalk in much the same way as you deal with an artichoke. It may be a rather time consuming affair but it is none the less an agreeable one.

Another salt marsh plant, but one which also brings us back to the shingle beaches and even cliffs, is sea purslane, a low shrubby perennial which enjoys well drained 'edge' country. The small silvery-white leaves are fleshy, and so too is some of the stem. These are the parts to boil. If you care to, you may chew and swallow the fresh leaves raw. They are a bit salty, but on a hot day the moisture is better than no water at all.

Use the asparagus technique with the young shoots of sea holly, which is a close relative of one of the globe artichokes; the large fleshy roots were used in Elizabethan times for sweetmeats. Colchester was famous for this trade, and in Cornwall, Borlase says, 'Our sands on the sea-shore afford some useful plants, of which the eryngo or sea-holly may be reckoned first; it is the Eryngium marinum of herbalists: its root, for excellent syrup, and candying, is universally acknowledged to be a great restorative. It grows in great plenty on the loose dry sands above full sea mark, where the sea never reaches. Having transplanted eryngo from the beach into a light, sandy, sunny part of my garden, I found it to thrive very well.'

Seaweed provides us with an abundance of edible food, if not very exciting gastronomically. In Japan and China it has been eaten for a very long time, but to a lesser extent in Europe and North America. It has always been remote island communities which have made the greatest use of the easily available and nutritious weed. It is rich in vitamins A, B1 and C. Weight for weight, some species contain more than half as much vitamin C as oranges. Indeed, it has been said that Eskimos get half of their vitamin C requirements from seaweed.

Raw seaweeds are perfectly edible, but unenjoyable. Boiling is highly recommended. Sea lettuce is one of the easily collected and certainly good looking table species. It is a green weed found at all times of the year attached to stones or rock, and the name is a good clue for identification. Collect a good deal, pick off the little dark stem pieces, clean and wash, boil for twenty minutes with salt and a little lemon or vinegar. Strain, chop and serve like cabbage. The taste, which is not perhaps one of the great experiences, is something like cabbage. (And I do not mean to decry cabbage, which I love!)

It has to be admitted that sea lettuce is an inferior substitute for laver, a much more important and widely used seaweed. It grows in the same sort of places and looks something like sea lettuce, but it has a rich rosy purple colour, which fades to olive green and darkens when it is dry. Known as laverbread in North Devon and South Wales, it is greatly enjoyed by anyone with good taste buds, although it is much reviled by the ignorant who call it a revolting mess. Leave them be, and try it. It needs careful washing. Boil it with a little vinegar. Strain and press well, then make into cakes which you roll in oatmeal and fry. Eat it with bacon and eggs and life will take a turn for the better. It is full of iron and all sorts of goodness, and is supposed to be good for rheumatism and hangovers. In Ireland they call it sloke.

Open sand flats: ideal cockling ground. The quantity of life underneath belies the surface calm.

One of the red seaweeds, carragheen, is the most important as a food product. It is normally a purple red, but may turn green in strong sun. Known also as 'Irish Moss', it can be processed to provide natural gums or mucilages with gelling properties, and is not easily replaced by synthetic products. In Ireland and in the Hebrides, carragheen is an important export, while it is used at home for the preparation of jellies, or where gelatinous material is required. A weak infusion may be used as a beverage, but only with the addition of a suitable strong flavouring I suspect. It is supposed to be good for bronchitis. In preparation it is washed and spread out in the sun to dry and bleach for a couple of weeks. Apart from its food value, one kind of carragheen is used to prepare a size for dressing manilla ropes and linen.

Dulse and pepper-dulse are used as vegetables, dried in the sun, rolled and chewed as a tobacco, and in Scotland the hot biting taste fits it for a condiment.

The seaweeds provide food for a great number of animals, and these in turn provide delicacies for man. The best hunting is on the lower levels of the beach, in shallow water and in tidal pools, and the quarry is anything from the humble periwinkle to the noble lobster. Remember that the principle of good farming, i.e. conservation, is to make sure that there will be a good crop next year as well as this, so never 'fish out' an area. Eat some; leave a good breeding stock. But seashore life is prolific, and danger to populations is more likely to come from large-scale commercial overfishing and the various forms of 'development' than from small depredations for our own table.

I am sometimes asked how I can bring myself to eat seashore creatures with apparent enjoyment when at the same time I profess an interest and respect for them. The answer is very simple. I go to the beach as a member of a predatory species which has business there. And the relationship between a predator and his prey is a healthy one with benefits for both participants, in the long run. A very much less admirable attitude to the seashore community, or any other for that matter, is that which regards it as a kind of sideshow or entertainment; something to be politely wondered at on a Sunday afternoon.

Shellfish tend to be found in enormous numbers, and in turn they support enormous numbers of predatory sea animals, birds, and of course, man. Take mussels for instance. A mussel bed covering one acre produces 10,000lb of meat a year with a calorific value of 3 million. Compare this with the average yield of one acre of pasture land, which produces 100lb, with a calory count of 120,000. Unfortunately from our point of view, mussels are highly susceptible to contamination, and it is only too easy to enjoy a plateful and follow it with an attack of gastro-enteritis, or even, in extreme cases, paralytic poisoning. The problem is that the mussels concentrate in themselves a poison derived from a tiny plankton animal called *Gonyaulax*. At certain times of the year there is a 'red tide' caused by a population explosion—a bloom—of these tiny animals, and they release a toxic agent which is now known as saxitoxin. These 'red tides' often occur at the same time as spectacular displays of luminescence of the sea at night. If in addition to these signs, you happen to notice an unusual number of dead animals, such as sand eels or birds, on the shore, it would certainly be wise to avoid eating shellfish. And if in any doubt it is as well to boil the molluscs for extra time, since this reduces the amount of toxin in the meat. A certain amount is concentrated in the cooking liquor, so this is always best discarded. Recent research at the University of California at Berkeley has unravelled the chemical structure of saxitoxin and it seems possible that public health authorities will soon be able to regulate the sale of shellfish in such a manner as to avoid danger.

Common shellfish or fish poisoning is usually caused by eating fish which has begun to decompose. These foods spoil very quickly, and the answer is to eat them fresh, and cook well. But if you are unfortunate enough to get smitten, then drink sea water and make yourself vomit.

After that catalogue of horrors it may seem unwise ever to eat anything from the shore. However, I only want to sound a note of caution before going on to say that almost any animal you take alive from a beach and rocky shore is edible. But cook well and do not eat anything raw. All molluscs—marine snails and bivalves—are good to eat; all crustaceans are good to eat; many echinoderms are good.

Friday is, of course, the traditional day for eating fish, and in many parts of the country Good Friday is a traditional day for going to the seashore and gathering a shellfish tea. Especially is this true of Cornwall, where the holy day was formerly kept more as a feast than a fast. Every vehicle was engaged long beforehand to take parties to their favourite collecting ground. Labourers in inland parishes walked to the nearest sea port to gather winkles. The practice goes back at least as far as the days of Queen Anne, and is known as 'trigging'.

In Devon, at any lunchtime which coincides with a low tide, there is a happy party of girls from the Dartmouth Pottery taking buckets onto the foreshore of Warfleet Creek, collecting the periwinkles which cluster in rich profusion on the flat slatey stones.

Cockles are less liable to pollution than mussels, presumably because they inhabit clean sandy beaches away from the sewer outfalls and polluted estuaries favoured by their less fortunate mates. They are collected in vast numbers. Cockle gatherers rake the sand and in taking the marketable specimens, leave the small ones to the tender mercies of predators like starfish and whelks, gulls, oystercatchers, flatfish and sea currents. Yet the splendid cockle survives in uncountable numbers.

On St Martin's Island in the Scillies, Bernard Bond and I used to harness the horse and go down to the sand flats at low water and harrow the beach for cockles from end to end. Then wash the bucketful in the sea. Back home to wash them in fresh water. Then wash them again. Then put them back in the bucket covered with water and a handful of salt for a couple of hours. Time for them to 'spit out the grit'. Then boil them for six minutes, when the cooked meat drops away from the shells. Wash again, and, best of all, eat them. Or maybe salt them or preserve in vinegar for another day. Marvellous. I can remember every moment of those long days, hot and salty.

Most cocklers collect them with a short-handled rake. In Morecambe Bay I believe they tread the sand with bare feet to bring cockles to the surface, and I would very much like to see them doing it, for this is an exact parallel to the way herring gulls go cockling. Incidentally, never eat a cockle you discover on the surface of the sand, there must be something wrong. The season begins in March, but is best from June onwards.

There are some cockle-like bivalves, which taste much the same and are treated the same way. Blunt tellins live in coarse sand and shell gravel at moderate depths, they are common, and may be cast ashore in large numbers after a storm. They are perfectly good to eat then, but collect them straightaway. They are related to the sand gaper (see page 37), a true shore species which is very common and much neglected as a food. It is the American soft-shelled clam, famous in connection with Boy Scout clam bakes in that country. It prefers shallow sand or sandy mud bottoms, and you can locate it by its squirting protest as you walk near. But all squirters are not clams. The excellent razorshell gives itself away by the same token. Digging them out with a spade is the standard method, but in the Channel Islands they put salt on their tails. There is a great deal of good white meat in the muscle of a razorshell.

Oysters hardly come within the scope of this book, for they are not wild beasts at all, but cultivated and strictly protected by law. So if you fancy a dozen, go and speak to the owner of the bed first. You are unlikely to find any that are 'lost', because they live below low-water mark. Equally you are unlikely to find the other noble shellfish, the scallop. Scallops are gregarious beasts which favour beds of clean firm sand, living in thousands at a depth of anything from 60 to 500ft. In some places, like Salcombe and Plymouth Sound, they can be collected from the bottom using aqualung gear, but mostly they are dredged up by inshore fishermen. Even if you are unlikely to find them on the beach, it is worth making friends with a fisherman just for the joy of getting some fresh scallops. Discard the black portion, poach them in the shell, and make a butter sauce with shallots and chopped parsley. And get a bottle of muscadet or cider to go with them.

Perhaps the nearest thing in quality to an oyster or a scallop which the beachcomber is likely to achieve, is an ormer. Related to the famous American abalone, you will have to go to the Channel Islands to find one. A large succulent limpet, it is a prized dish to Channel Islanders. The beautiful shell is very flattened, with an elegant series of openings just inside the edge. It lives under rocks and stones at low-water mark.

Coming down to earth again, or rather to a typical rock pool, the common limpet is palatable. In the Channel Islands they cook and eat them on the shore, covering them with a heap of straw set on fire about twenty minutes before dinner time.

Sea urchins are more popular in Mediterranean countries than in Northern Europe, nowadays, but in the past the roes of the big ones, *Echinus esculentus*, were eaten, either raw, boiled, baked or steamed.

There are some general rules for shellfish treatment. Put them in fresh water with salt for anything up to twelve hours in order to encourage them to expel waste products and grit. If after this time any bivalves are in an 'open' condition, throw them away, but not in the dustbin. Put them somewhere, like the garden, where they will decompose and enrich the soil, thus recycling instead of wasting them. Cover them with water and boil, for not less than six minutes (cockles) and three minutes (periwinkles). Extract meat, eat as it comes, or cut up the white meat, roll in breadcrumbs and fry. In the case of mussels, steam, boil, or bake in shell. They make good stews, delicious with sea beet.

The RSPCA say you should put shellfish in cold water and bring it to the boil, but no one seems very confident about the kindest way to kill them. They have no brain or central nervous system so it is difficult to assess their pain reactions. But I feel strongly that the best thing is to drop them straight into boiling water and a quick death. Crustaceans do have well developed nervous systems and must therefore be able to feel pain. So it is vital to kill them efficiently and with compassion. Fortunately they are very easy to deal with. They can live for long periods in fresh water, so just putting them in the fresh cold water and bringing them to the boil is a cruel act. Put them into fiercely boiling water and they are killed instantly. It is no good being squeamish about these things. More people have been cruel to the animals which they profess to 'love' than bears thinking about. Crustaceans may be steamed, boiled, roasted, or baked. Prawns and shrimps should be boiled for about three minutes; crabs and lobsters twenty to forty-five minutes according to size. Remove the dark-grey gill 'fingers' of a crab, but you can eat everything else.

Fish should never be picked up from the beach and eaten, however good they may look. The flesh deteriorates rapidly, and it is vital that the fish should be fresh. Good fish is firm, not soft and flabby. On the whole salt-water fish are free from harmful parasites, but anyway they are sterilised by cooking. Fish meat is very little different from mammal meat, just protein and water, but it has a high iodine and vitamin D content. Maybe you get yours from an inshore or sport fisherman, or from a beach netter, or by casting from the beach, or by stalking in a rock pool, but please do them the favour of killing them as soon as you have caught them, by a blow on the head, or by breaking the neck. I am diffident about the continual harping on this subject, but so many people who are kind and warm-hearted act in a brutally cruel way towards fish and other 'cold-blooded' beasts.

Having achieved a dead fish, clean it by inserting a knife blade at the anal opening and cutting forward to the head. Cut off head, gills and tail if you want to (it is not necessary). Draw out entrails in one fell swoop. Keep liver and roe if you like it, but make sure the gall bladder does not burst; remove it whole. Cut blood vessels, against backbone, and flush and clean away streaks of blood. Do not clean blood away with your thumbnail, because of the danger of blood poisoning. Scrape scaly fish underwater—the scales are less inclined to fly about.

Mackerel are the most likely fish with which you will be dealing, and they are about the most delicious. Split and bake them, or boil in sea water. Or you can roast them on a green stick over the hot embers of a fire, or roast them in the embers using aluminium foil (or layers of green leaves and mud if you are really playing at Crusoe), alongside the potatoes. The de-luxe method of smoking is to use an Abu smoker, a stove which produces golden, smoky-tasting fish very quickly.

Smoking the vagrant way is less efficient, but more fun. Build a stick-grate 3–4ft above a slow burning fire, and lay split fish or strips on the lattice. Do not let the fire get so hot it cooks the fish or draws out the juices, the smoke rising from the smouldering wood is sufficient. Continue smoking until the fish is brittle. In the case of small fish, leave their heads on and hang them over the fire by threading a stick through the gills. Avoid oily woods which blacken the food and give it a nasty flavour. The finished product should keep for a long time. Chew it raw, or cook as required.

For preparing fish we need water, salt and a fire. So let us just summarise the important points. Even if you have a nearby source of fresh water from a stream, be suspicious and boil it for five minutes before drinking. You should be able to get fresh water from any beach, provided you have plenty of time. Dig a shallow well, above high-water mark, not too deep. Line the pit with a plastic sheet and put a few biggish stones in there. Dew will collect in the bottom of the plastic. Salt water, of course, is in plentiful supply, since the main character of the sea is its saltiness. (There are many other chemicals in its make-up, with traces of all the elements. In coastal waters, where the influence of rivers and land run-off is great, the salinity is lower than in the ocean.)

We shall need salt. Very often it is sufficient to use sea water for cooking, but it is very easy to prepare dry salt from sea water for use not only on the beach but at home. All you do is boil sea water. But I must warn you that the amount of steam produced is phenomenal, and if you do it indoors you end up with a very wet kitchen. One gallon of sea water, which may take well over an hour to boil away, leaves you with a residue of delicious salt crystals which will fill a teacup about two-thirds full. Well, it impresses your friends, if nothing else.

All these foods taste a good deal better if you prepare them on the beach. That is not just romantic eyewash, because there is nothing so good as fresh fish. So you need to make a cooking fire. Find a dry sheltered spot out of the wind. Scoop out the sand or use a couple of big bits of drift wood to form a fire place. Use dry dead wood to start the fire. (Dry wood snaps, damp wood bends.) Have plenty of wood standing by to keep the fire going. Start small and build up, remembering that a fire needs plenty of air. Do not put too much fuel on too soon.

In rain, build under a rock shelf, and be extra sure to have enough dry wood ready before you start. Wet wood will burn on a fire once it is burning well. The resinous pitch in pine knots burns fiercely even while it is damp, so it can be useful on damp days. Hard woods are slow burning and a shocking waste on a fire. Soft woods burn fast and hot, but are soon gone.

A small fire is always the most useful one, many people get a great bonfire going, then find they cannot get near enough to cook anything. Crisscross sticks burn down soonest. This is the best technique because, for cooking, your object is to get a bed of glowing embers; flames are not so effective.

Now you are ready to cook. Spear a fish on a green stick and cantilever it out over the fire. Keep it as close to the embers as possible, then it will harden quickly on the surface, thus keeping in the juices. For baking, dig a pit in the sand. Wrap your fish in wet leaves or mud or clay. Pile on hot embers, cover with a few inches of sand. Leave for about an hour.

Beach cooking is a great joy. Sail to a remote and sheltered cove in the late afternoon, swim or paddle ashore in the dinghy and then search around for some firewood. With a strong little fire going you are free to go and prepare the fish down at the water's edge, giving it a good wash in the sea. Then the smell of the cooking and the warmth of the fire as the sun goes down; the sense of well-being and harmony with the rest of the world is rare and memorable however many times you do it.

And if some guilt-ridden misery tries to spoil it by suggesting you are being beastly to the animals, brace yourself and smile kindly, offering him a plateful of grilled mackerel.

5 The horrors of the beach

Shore walking and wading is not without its hazards, but it is a good deal safer than walking along any road.

The most likely danger is that of treading on a piece of glass, and on any popular beach it is probably only safe to walk in shoes. Even the remotest places suffer, though, because of course bottles are blown ashore and break with the waves on the tideline. Although the beach soon grinds them down to size there is a danger period. Watch out for nails in timber wreck, too. I once had a nail which went right through a pair of heavy gumboots and into my heel; it was painful for a long time afterwards.

Oil, in liquid form, and in the tarry ball version is a real menace on beaches nowadays, and I think we must assume that it will be a continuing problem for some time to come, even though there is a perfectly practical method, called the 'load-on-top' system, for avoiding the sort of operational oil spillage that comes from tank-cleaning or discharge of ballast water. All the major oil companies use load-on-top, and this means more than 80 per cent of all tankers, but the remainder do not, largely because independent refineries will not accept salt water with their crude oil cargoes. They will have to do this when rules drawn up by IMCO, the UN agency that deals with these matters, have been adopted by all the member countries—and the quicker the better. There is still the risk of accidental spillage or collision, while some oil gets into the sea from dry cargo ships' bilges or even from wartime wrecks that have begun to break up.

On the small scale, eucalyptus oil (from the chemist's shop) will clean your body, your clothes or your carpets with ease and, incidentally, you can use it safely on a dog's paws. But on the large scale, when a beach is covered with oil, it is not so easy to know what to do. If the oil is in the form of tarry balls, then it can be collected and burned. Burying it actually slows down the rate of disintegration, though it may make it less of a nuisance for the time being. The fact is that if you do nothing and leave the oil where it is, micro-organisms which enjoy eating it will multiply and reduce it over a period of a few months. If they are properly controlled, dispersants can be sprayed on the oil to break it into small droplets. In the *Torrey Canyon* disaster, as much or more damage was done to inter-tidal flora and fauna by millions of gallons of toxic dispersant recklessly spread on the beaches, and they took two years or more to recover. At least the affair prompted research, and nowadays dispersants have been produced which have a very low toxicity. It is still necessary to use them correctly, and in the right places and, above all, to make sure they are thoroughly mixed with the oil. Contingency plans are also much better developed, with stocks of equipment kept round the coasts, so when the *Pacific Glory* and the *Allegro* collided in the Channel in 1970, for example, with a loss of some 5,000 tons of oil, practically none reached the shore.

There is a whole world of horror in the very name 'quicksands', yet the danger is not serious if you deal with the situation calmly. Get to know the local danger spots, if any, and avoid them. Avoid a patch of mud covered with slimy green algae in the midst of clean mud. If by mischance you do start to sink, don't thrash about, but lean gently forward with spread arms, then 'swim' your way back to safety. Keep your body horizontal and spread your weight about.

At the very lowest part of a sandy beach, the area uncovered by spring tides, there is a fish which buries itself in sand with only the top of its head and its dorsal fin visible. This is the lesser weever, which has a poisonous gland at the base of the dorsal fin. Step on it, and it will inject a poisonous secretion which will cause painful swellings. It is a true sand-dweller, preying on shrimps, and widely distributed in shallow coastal waters, though more common in the south.

Stingrays do occur as far north as 51°, so they are a possible danger, and the electric ray is not uncommon in the English Channel, and has been taken in waters as far north as Scotland. Rays are beautifully adapted to 'flying' underwater but when they lie on the sea bed they are very difficult to see. They frequent sand and mud bottoms, and have tail stingers that can drive through your foot, leaving a wound liable to infection. The stingray has a serrated poison spine on the back of the tail. The electric ray can give a shock severe enough to knock a fully grown man down if he accidentally steps on it.

So do not walk in too genteel a manner in shallow sandy water at low tide. Poke about ahead of you and shuffle along causing a commotion. That way, weevers and rays and all fierce beasts will know you are coming and prudently go somewhere else.

Jellyfish need watching, The Portuguese man-o'-war has long tentacles that produce painful stings and severe swelling which may last several hours. The greatest danger is that it may cause a swimmer to panic or get cramp. Difficult though it may be in practice, the correct procedure is to relax. Once ashore, the prompt application of ammonia will relieve the pain. Native, but still uncommon, stinging jellyfish are *Cyanea capillata*, a gaudy east-coast beast of blue and violet, hung with eight bunches of tentacles, and *Chrysaora isosceles*, which is anything from 4–18in across, milk-white with a brown central spot and brown radii, found in the south and west. The commonest jellyfish of all, *Aurelia*, with its four purple-violet rings, does have stinging tentacles but they are hardly powerful enough to affect human skin.

Conger eels can bite and lash you with their tails; octopuses can bite and entwine you with their tentacles, but as they are mostly concerned to give you a wide berth it is unfair to class them as horrors. Congers may be 6ft long and weigh 100lb, so treat them with respect. An octopus that might be big enough to be dangerous lives in the ocean depths, a very good place for him too.

In case you feel a shark or killer whale might carry you off, it is worth recording that no one has ever been killed or eaten in British waters by either of these creatures. Some shark anglers have been hurt in the process of 'landing' their catch, but I think perhaps they deserve it, for sharking is a feeble sport.

Any or all of these hazards may spoil your day, but the chances are slim. Ignoring all my own pious advice, I have leapt about on beaches and gone shrimping in shallow water for as many years as I can remember without anything worse than a few minor cuts and sunburn. Even if, one day, a weever gets me, I hope I will staunch the tears and take pleasure in observing the clever way he hides in the sand, spying on the shrimps. For both of us are at home in these places, and we are designed to live in long-term harmony with each other. Most wonderful of all, no matter how many shrimps he eats, or I eat in the whole of a lifetime, there will still be millions of shrimps and cockles and herring gulls and people to go on scavenging, wrecking and combing beaches.

Appendix I

Wreck law

The King shall have wreck of the sea throughout the realm.

17 Edward II c II, S I

In other words, finders are not keepers. Not legally, anyway. In fact it is not even very clear whether or not a wrecker has the right to be on the beach at all. The law relating to flotsam, jetsam and lagan is full of pitfalls and anomalies, but the basic premise is that all things found at sea or on the beach belong to somebody. Most of the foreshore is owned by the Crown, but not all of it. Lords of the manor have different rights in different parts of the country, and the records are full of exotic dispute.

The expression 'wreck' has been defined as property cast ashore after shipwreck or found in or on the shores of any tidal water. In addition the definition covers all 'derelict' articles, derelict being a term used to describe property, whether vessel or cargo, which has been abandoned without hope of recovery. From this it follows that most articles found on the shore or retrieved from the sea bed may fall within the definition of wreck.

Wreck is classified as either owned or unclaimed. In both cases the salvor has a duty to inform the Receiver of Wreck. With owned wreck he may claim salvage rights from the owner. In any dispute the Receiver acts as arbiter. Interference with wreck without permission of the owner involves liability to a penalty not exceeding £100. Removing parts of the wreck and not returning them to the owner incurs a penalty of double the value of the wreck.

In the case of unclaimed wreck, the Receiver enters the case in a register and this is known as 'opening a droit'. Unclaimed after one year, the property reverts to the Crown and is sold. In this case the salvor usually gets one third of the proceeds, although there is no legal basis for this figure which may vary according to the danger of the salvage operation, the degree of skill involved, etc.

Articles which do not come within the definition of wreck come in the same category as lost property. Deck cargo, when washed overboard, becomes lost property, even though the cargo may finish up on the shore. (There is an anomaly in the case of fishing gear. If it is lost overboard it *does* constitute wreck, although no shipwreck need be involved.)

Navigation marks, buoys, etc., when adrift, are not wreck, but lost property, and this same protection applies to anything found within the confines of a harbour or above MHWS level. The theft of lost property is dealt with as an act of common larceny.

Flotsam is wreck found floating at sea. Jetsam is wreck which has been cast overboard to lighten ship in peril. And lagan is wreck found cast ashore.

So it is clear that, legally, all wreck must be reported. If the property has a likely value of £20 or more the Receiver (normally the local Customs Officer) must notify Lloyds. If the wreck is below a certain value, or perishable, and is unclaimed, the officer may sell it, an appropriate award being made to the salvor. The Receiver of Wreck has wide powers. He may requisition vessels or vehicles. He has legal powers to enter private land if he suspects that an offence has been committed. It is his duty to suppress attempts at plunder. And, incidentally, it is an offence even to board a wrecked vessel without the consent of either the Receiver or the owner.

Certain wrecks are of archaeological interest, and if you discover anything which might come in this category it should be left undisturbed and reported to the Council for Nautical Archaeology (contacted through the National Maritime Museum at Greenwich), although the Receiver of Wreck must be informed first.

Appendix II

Key to British whales and dolphins

In using this key the inquirer should in all cases begin with the first bracket (1), and should decide between the two alternatives there presented. He will thus be referred either to bracket 2 or to bracket 7; and by continuing the process of deciding between two alternatives he will sooner or later arrive at a definite result. Suppose that a large whale with very strong teeth in its lower jaw, has been found: of the two alternatives given in the first bracket, the second must be chosen because teeth are present. The inquirer is thus referred to bracket 7, the consideration of which shows at once that the specimen must be a Sperm Whale.

1 { Whalebone present on palate. Teeth absent. Lower jaw very wide, its halves arched outwards *Whalebone Whales* 2
Whalebone absent. Teeth present, though sometimes concealed beneath the gum. Lower jaw narrow, at least in front *Toothed Whales* 7

WHALEBONE WHALES

2 { Lower surface of throat not grooved. No back fin. Mouth and upper border of lower lip much arched. Whalebone blades long, up to 6–9ft *Atlantic Right Whale*
Lower surface of throat with numerous parallel grooves 3

3 { Flippers extremely long, nearly one-third the length of the animal, sometimes white externally, with a scalloped lower margin *Humpback*
Flippers much less than one-third the total length, not scalloped below *Rorquals* 4

4 { Whalebone, yellowish white or slate-coloured, or both 5
Whalebone, black or nearly black 6

5 { Size, up to 70ft. Whalebone, yellow and slate-coloured, except at the front of the right side, where it is white; its hairy fringes, white or yellowish. Tail-flukes white below *Common Fin Whale*
Size, up to 30ft. Whalebone and its hairy fringes, all white or yellowish. A white region on outer side of flipper *Lesser Rorqual*

6 {
Size, up to 85ft. Whalebone very black, with coarse black hairs
Blue Whale

Size, up to 50ft. Whalebone mostly dark, with very fine, white, curling, silky hairs, Tail-flukes not white below *Sei Whale*
}

TOOTHED WHALES

7 {
Tip of lower jaw well behind foremost limit of head — 8
Tip of lower jaw at about same level as tip of snout — 9
}

8 {
Size that of a large whale to about 60ft *Sperm Whale*
Size that of a dolphin to about 12ft *Pigmy Sperm Whale*
}

9 {
Back fin absent — 10
Back fin present — 11
}

10 {
Head short, with prominent 'forehead'. Colour greyish, with black spots or mottlings. Either without visible teeth (females), or with a tusk-lie tooth, several feet long, spirally twisted, projecting forwards from the front of the upper jaw (males), exceptionally with two spiral tusks *Narwhal*

Colour, white all over (greyish-brown in young individuals), 8–10 pairs of teeth in each jaw *White Whale*
}

11 {
Teeth confined to the lower jaw, or apparently absent — 12
Teeth in both jaws — 16
}

12 {
Back fin large, near middle of body. Teeth 2–7 pairs, at front end of lower jaw *Risso's Dolphin*
Back fin considerably behind middle of body. Front end of jaws narrow. Two grooves on throat *Whales of the 'Bottle-nosed' type* — 13
}

13 {
Size, large, up to 25–30ft. Distance from tip of snout to blowhole one-fifth to one-seventh the total length. 'Forehead' very prominent. Teeth (one to two pairs) at tip of lower jaw, usually concealed *Bottle-nosed Whale*

Distance from tip of snout to blowhole less than one-seventh the total length — 14
}

14 {
Size, large, up to 26ft. Distance from tip of snout to blowhole one-tenth to one-eighth the total length. 'Forehead' not specially prominent. Teeth one pair at tip of lower jaw, massive in males (diameter 1in), concealed in females *Cuvier's Whale*

Size smaller, not exceeding 20ft. Beak long — 15
}

15 {
Length about 15ft. Colour mostly black, usually with white marks. One pair of teeth at middle of length of lower jaw, conspicuous and triangular in males, concealed in females *Sowerby's Whale*

Size rather larger. Colour not satisfactorily known. One pair of teeth at tip of lower jaw, conspicuous and flattened sideways in males, concealed in females *True's Beaked Whale**
}

*In addition to Sowerby's Whale and True's Beaked Whale, the two species of *Mesoplodon* mentioned in bracket 14, it is probable that a third species (*M. europaeus*), perhaps reaching 20ft in length, will be recorded as British. Its external appearance is not well known.

16 {	Size large, 15–30ft in adults. Teeth 8–13in each jaw	17
	Seldom exceeding 12ft, usually less than 9ft. Teeth not more than $\frac{1}{2}$in in diameter, more than 15 pairs	19

17 {
'Forehead' greatly swollen, overhanging the tip of the very short beak. Flippers narrow, about one-fifth of the total length. Colour black, with only a small amount of white on lower surface. Teeth 8–12 pairs in each jaw, less than $\frac{1}{2}$in in diameter   *Pilot-Whale*
'Forehead' not prominent. Teeth, 10–13 pairs in each jaw, at least $\frac{3}{4}$in in diameter   18

18 {
Colour conspicuously black and white (or yellow). Flippers broad, not pointed. Teeth about 1in in diameter   *Killer*
Colour black all over. Flippers narrow and pointed. Teeth as in the Killer   *False Killer*

19 {
Size up to $5\frac{1}{2}$ft. Teeth about 21–24 pairs in each jaw, flattened sideways, with spade-shaped crowns. Beak not distinguishable   *Common Porpoise*
Size larger, teeth conical, the crowns not flattened sideways. Beak distinct   20

20 {
Length up to 12ft. Beak about 3in long in middle line. Teeth large, 20–25 pairs in each jaw; diameter, $\frac{3}{8}$–$\frac{1}{2}$in   *Bottle-nosed Dolphin*
Teeth not exceeding $\frac{1}{4}$in in diameter   21

21 {
Beak about 2 in long in middle line. Length, 9–10ft   22
Beak up to 6in in middle line. Teeth, 40–50 pairs in each jaw, about $\frac{1}{10}$in in diameter. Length up to 7ft   23

22 {
Upper lip white. Dark colour of flippers continuous with that of body, their lower margin not much curved. Teeth, about 25 pairs in each jaw; diameter, $\frac{1}{4}$in   *White-beaked Dolphin*
Upper lip black. Flippers, with strongly curved lower margin, arising from white part of body, usually connected with dark part by a narrow dark streak. A conspicuous white region on each side, behind the back fin. Teeth, 30–40 pairs in each jaw; diameter, $\frac{3}{16}$in   *White-sided Dolphin*

23 {
A well-marked, narrow dark band of pigment extending from the eye along the flank and curving down to the vent, with a subsidiary branch in the region of the flipper insertion   *Euphrosyne Dolphin*
This band wanting, but an arrangement of yellowish, white and dark bands on the sides of the body   *Common Dolphin*

Reference sources

Those books marked with an asterisk are strongly recommended for the wrecker's library. The Collins' *Pocket Guide to the Sea Shore*, by John Barrett and C. M. Yonge is virtually indispensable and is by far the best book for field identification, For birds, the most useful identification book is Collins' *Field Guide to the Birds of Britain and Europe*, by Peterson, Mountfort and Hollom.

Admiralty, *Aircrew Survival Handbook* (1963)
——, *Notices to Mariners* (annual summary, 1972)
Anon, *A Brief History of Amber* (Konisberg, 1913)
——, 'A Guide to Fish Marks', *J Cons Perm Int Explor Mer* 30 no 1 (1965)
Ashton, J., *Curious Creatures in Zoology* (1890)
*Barrett, J. H. and Yonge, C. M., *Collins Pocket Guide to the Sea Shore* (1960)
Bateman, J. A., *Animal Traps and Trapping* (Newton Abbot, 1971)
Bergen, F. D. (ed), *Animal and Plant Lore collected from the oral tradition of the English speaking folk* (1899)
Bolster, G. C., *Mackerel of the South West* (1971)
Bonner, W. N., *Seal Deaths in Cornwall, Autumn 1969* (1971)
Borlase, W., *The Natural History of Cornwall* (Oxford, 1758)
Brightman, F. H., *The Oxford Book of Flowerless Plants* (Oxford, 1966)
Brongersma, L. D., *British Turtles* (1967)
Burton, J., *The Oxford Book of Insects* (Oxford, 1968)
Carr, A. P., 'Shingle spit and river mouth: short term dynamics', *Inst Br Geographers*, publication 36
Casanova, R., *Fossil Collecting* (1960)
Carruthers, J. N., '"Bottle Post" and other Drifts', *J Inst Nav* 9 no 3 (1956)
——, 'Floating Messages', *PLA Monthly*, 44 no 525
*Chapman, V. J. *Coastal Vegetation* (1964)
——, *Seaweeds and their Uses* (1970)
Clark, A. M., *Starfishes* (1968)
Countryside Commission, *The Coasts of England and Wales: measurement of use, protection and development* (1968)
——, *Nature Conservation at the Coast* (1969)
——, *The Coastal Heritage* (1970)
Courtney, M. A., *Cornish Feasts and Folklore* (Penzance, 1890)
Cox, I. (ed), *The Scallop* (1957)
Craighead, F. C. and J. J., *How to Survive on Land and Sea* (US Navy, 1970)
Cruickshank, C., *Lenten Fare and Food for Fridays* (1959)
Dance, S. P., *Seashells* (1971)

Dare, P. J., *The Breeding and Wintering Populations of Oystercatchers in the British Isles* (1966)

Eales, N. B., *The Littoral Fauna of Great Britain* (Cambridge, 1950)

Ellis, C., *The Pebbles on the Beach* (1954)

Eltringham, S. K., *Life in Mud and Sand* (1971)

*Fisher, J. and Lockley, R. M., *Sea Birds* (1954)

Forsyth, W. S., *Common British Seashells* (1961)

Francis, J. G. ,*Beach Rambles in Search of Seaside Pebbles and Crystals* (1861)

Fraser, F. C., *Report on Cetacea* (1953)

*Fraser, F. C., *British Whales, Dolphins and Porpoises* (1969)

Friedrich, H., *Marine Biology* (1969)

Giddings, *Driftwood and Arctic Currents* (Pennsylvania, 1952)

Gill, C., et al., *The Wreck of the 'Torrey Canyon'* (Newton Abbot, 1967)

Gosse, P. H., *A Naturalist's Rambles on the Devonshire Coast* (1853)

Green, J., *The Biology of Estuarine Animals* (1968)

Hale, M. E., *The Biology of Lichens* (1967)

*Hardy, Sir A., *The Open Sea* (1956)

*——, *Fish and Fisheries* (1959)

*Hepburn, I. *Flowers of the Coast* (1966)

Hole, C. (ed), *Encyclopaedia of Superstitions* (1961)

*Hollom, P. A. D., *The Popular Handbook of British Birds* (1968)

Houghton, Rev W., *Sea-side Walks of a Naturalist with his Children* (1889)

Hulme, F. E., *Natural History, Lore and Legend* (1895)

ICI, 'Restriction of sand movement and coastal erosion by artificial seaweed', *Artificial Seaweed News Sheet* (1969)

Inwards, R., *Weather Lore* (1950)

Iselin, C. O. D., 'Preliminary report on long-term variation in transport of Gulf Stream', *Pap Phys Oceanog and Met* 8 no 1 (1940)

Iverson, E. S., *Farming the Edge of the Sea* (1968)

Jolliffe, J. P., 'An experiment designed to compare the relative rates of movement of different sizes of beach pebble'. *Proc Geologists Assoc* 75 part 1 (1964)

Jones, P. H., 'Ornithological Beachcombing in Merioneth', *Nature in Wales* (Sept 1971)

Kidson, C. and Carr, A. P., 'The movement of shingle over the sea bed close in-shore', *The Geog J* 125 parts 3–4

Kidson, C., 'The growth of sand and shingle spits across estuaries'. *Annals of Geomorphology* (1963)

Kunz, G. F., 'Folklore of Precious Stones', *Mem Internat Congress of Anthropology* (1894)

Lawford, A. L., Cdr RN, 'Postscript to Operation Post Card' *Trident*, (Sept 1956)

Leach, Maria (ed), *Standard Dictionary of Folklore, Mythology and Legend* (New York 1950)

Lewis, J. R., *The Ecology of Rocky Shores* (1964)

Leyel, C. F., *Culpeper's Herbal* (1947)

MAFF, 'Studies with the Woodhead Sea-Bed Drifter' (1965)

Marshall, S. M. and Orr, A. P., *The Fertile Sea* (1969)

Masefield, G. B., et al, *The Oxford Book of Food Plants* (Oxford, 1969)

Mills, D. H., *The Distribution and Food of the Cormorant in Scottish Inland Waters* (1965)

Ministry of Defence, *Underwater Handbook* (1971)

Moore, S. A., *A History of the Foreshore and Law relating thereto* (1888)

——, *The History of Law and Fisheries* (1903)

McCollum, J. P. K., et al, 'An epidemic of mussel poisoning in North East England', *The Lancet* (5 Oct 1968)

Newton, L., *A Handbook of the British Seaweeds* (1931)

——, *Seaweed Utilisation* (1951)

Norman, D., et al, *The Oxford Book of Invertebrates* (Oxford, 1971)

Norman, J. R., *A History of Fishes* (1960)

*Peterson, R., et al, *A Field Guide to the Birds of Britain and Europe* (1966)

Ranwell, D. S., *World Resources of Spartina* (Oxford, 1967)

Richardson, Sir J., *The Museum of Natural History—Fishes* (1862)

Ritchie, C. I. A., *Carving Shells and Cameos and other Marine Products* (1970)

Rolfe, M. S., 'Escallops off Plymouth' *MAFF* (1969)

Russell, A. S. and Yonge, C. M., *The Seas* (1963)

Shepherd, W., *The Living Landscape of Britain* (1963)

Slijper, E. J., *Whales* (1962)

Smith, J. E. (ed), '*Torrey Canyon' Pollution and Marine Life* (Cambridge, 1968)

Sowerby, A. de C., *A Naturalist's Holiday by the Sea* (1923)

*Steers, J. A., *The Sea Coast* (1954)

——, *The Coastline of England and Wales* (Cambridge, 1969)

—— (ed), *Introduction to Coastline Development* (1971)

Street, P., *Shell Life on the Seashore* (1961)

Swainson, Rev C., *A Handbook of Weather Folklore* (1873)

Taylor, J. N., 'Illustrated guide to the Severn Fishery Collection' (*Gloucester Folk Museum*, 1953)

*Tebble, N., *British Bivalve Seashells* (1966)

UFAW, *Humane Killing of Crabs and Lobsters* (1971)

Vaughan, R. W., *Aerial Survey of Seals in the Wash* (1972)

Vevers, H. G., *The British Seashore* (1954)

Watts, Capt O. M. (ed), *Reeds Nautical Almanac* (1972)

Williamson, G. C., *The Book of Amber* (1932)

Witherby, H. F., et al, *The Handbook of British Birds* (1952)

Yarrell, W., *A History of British Fishes* (1836)

*Yonge, C. M., *The Sea Shore* (1949)

Yonge, C. M., *Oysters* (1960)

Young, E. G. and McLachlan, J. C. (ed), *Proc 5th International Seaweed Symposium* (1965)

Zim. H. S. and Ingle, L., *Seashores* (New York, 1955)

Scientific names of plants and animals mentioned in the text

Albatross	*Diomedea sp.*
Barnacle, acorn	*Balanus sp.*
Barnacle, goose	*Lepas sp.*
Brittle star	Order OPHIUROIDEA
Buzzard	*Buteo buteo*
By-the-wind sailor	*Vellella spirans*
Carragheen	*Chondrus crispus*
Chough	*Pyrrhococora pyrrhocorax*
Cockle, dog	*Glycymeris glycymeris*
Cowrie, arctic	*Trivia arctica*
Cowrie, European	*Trivia monacha*
Crab, common hermit	*Eupaguras bernhardus*
Crab, edible	*Cancer pagurus*
Crab, long-clawed porcelain	*Porcellana longicornis*
Crab, shore	*Carcinus maenas*
Crab, spiny spider	*Maia squinado*
Clam, soft-shelled	*Mya arenaria*
Cuttle, little	*Sepiola atlantica*
Cuttlefish	*Sepia officinalis*
Dogfish, common	*Scyliorhinus canicula*
Dolphin, bottle-nosed	*Tursiops truncatus*
Dove, rock	*Columba livia*
Dulse	*Rhodymenia palmata*
Dunnock	*Prunella modularis*
Eel, conger	*Conger conger*
Eel grass	*Zostera marina*
Fennel	*Foeniculum vulgare*
Fox	*Vulpes vulpes*
Fulmar	*Fulmarus glacialis*
Gaper, sand	*Mya arenaria*
Glasswort	*Salicornia stricta*
Goose, barnacle	*Branta leucopsis*
Goose, brent	*Branta bernicla*
Gribble	*Limnoria lignorum*
Guillemot	*Uria aalge*
Gull, black-headed	*Larus redibund*
Gull, herring	*Larus argentatus*
Irish Moss	*Chondrus crispus*
Jackdaw	*Corvus monedula*
Kittiwake	*Rissa tridactyla*
Laver	*Porphyra umbilicalis*
Limpet, blue-rayed	*Patina pellucia*
Limpet, common	*Patella vulgata*
Limpet, slipper	*Crepidula fornicata*
Lobster	*Homarus vulgaris*
Lugworm	Family ARENICOLID.
Mackerel	*Scomber scombrus*
Mussel, common	*Mytilus edulis*
Narwhal	*Monodon monoceros*
Octopus, common	*Octopus vulgaris*
Orache	*Atriplex sp.*
Ormer	*Haliotis tuberculata*
Otter	*Lutra lutra*
Oyster, native	*Ostrea edulis*
Oystercatcher	*Haematopus ostralegu*
Pepper dulse	*Laurenicia pinnatifida*
Peregrine	*Falco perigrinus*
Periwinkle, common	*Littorina litto*
Pipit, rock	*Anthus spinoletta*
Plover, ringed	*Charadrius hiaticula*
Porpoise	*Phocaena phocaena*
Prawn, common	*Leander serratus*
Purslane, sea	*Halimione portucaloides*
Rabbit	*Oryctolagus cuniculus*
Raven	*Corvus corax*
Ray, electric	*Torpedo nobiliana*
Ray, sting	*Trygon pastinaca*
Razorbill	*Alca torda*
Razorshell	Family SOLENIDAE
Robin	*Erithacus rubecula*

Acknowledgements

I am grateful for help, advice, specimens and information to: the Keeper of Zoology, British Museum (Natural History); Dr J. N. Carruthers and the Librarian of the National Institute of Oceanography; the Librarian of the Marine Biological Association of the United Kingdom; Mr T. Williams of the Fisheries Laboratory, Lowestoft; especially I should like to record my appreciation of the help so freely given by Leslie Jackman and by Mr W. H. Williams, HM District Inspector of Fisheries, Plymouth, and Mr S. C. Lawrence, Head Receiver of Wreck, Devon and Cornwall.

And this is an appropriate place to record gratitude to my friend Ronald Lockley, who shipped me as crew when exploring the shores and remote islands of Pembrokeshire; and to Bernard Bond, who, as farmer-fisherman in the Isles of Scilly so generously gave his time and enthusiasm to showing me the mysteries of his trade.

Fort Bovisand   Tony Soper
Plymouth
Spring 1972

Index

Figures in heavy type refer to illustrations